I0839380

Short Course
Political Science

Klaus-Peter Saalbach

Verlag Dirk Koentopp

Saalbach, Klaus-Peter:
Short Course Political Science
Osnabrück: Verlag Dirk Koentopp, 2010
ISBN 978-3-938342-21-3

ISBN 978-3-938342-21-3

1. Preface

Political issues are relevant for everybody, but they are often complex and difficult to understand. Political Science provides theories and instruments to analyze these matters and it is useful to have at least a basic knowledge of this subject.

This book is intended to give a short and easy-to-read introduction to Political Science and is based on introductory courses at the University of Osnabrück in Northern Germany. The most important theories and debates are presented and a short overview on recent developments is given.

Topics are e.g. policy analysis, the motives for policy making, theory of government and governance, international relations, energy and security policy.

This book should not replace teaching books and the work with scientific literature, but may motivate the reader to learn more about this fascinating subject.

Table of Contents

List of Tables

2. The Analysis of Political Issues

2.1 What Does Politics Mean?

The word is derived from the classic Greek term **'polis'; (town)** which means 'public affairs'. The Romans used the terms **res privata** and **res publica** for private and public affairs, the word **republic** is derived from this.

From a formal point of view, there are three dimensions:
- Polity - the formal and institutional framework of a state (e.g. the constitution)
- Politics - the political process (e.g. voting procedures)
- Policy - the content (e.g. a new law)

For many people, politics is another word for selfishness, interests, pressures and profits and they ask why things could not be handled in an objective 'non-political' manner. But politics is more than this, because almost at any time the resources (time, people, money, environment and so on…) are too limited to satisfy all needs. Therefore, choices have to be made who will get how much (**allocation problem**) and as long as there is need for such choices, we will have political issues, even if the final decisions are fair.

2.2 Analysis Steps

2.2.1 Introduction

The general question is **what political actors do, why they do it and what difference it makes.** The term political actors indicates that not only governments can be politically relevant, there are many other groups as well, e.g. lobby organizations, associations, trade unions, and so on.

How can we analyze political issues?

You can analyze a political problem (e.g. unemployment-what can be done?) or a certain policy result (e.g. there was a new employment program-did this help?).

2.2.2 Some Practical Problems

In theory, political research is done carefully, systematically and step by step. However, if you work as an analyst, you have to live with a permanent lack of time, resources and money. Often analyses have to be done in a 'quick and dirty' manner. A true story: A friend was asked by his boss: "I need to talk about Dubai. *Write something* and give it to me *this afternoon*". Therefore, try to be simple, clear, focused, no frills.

The best way to get a deep insight into a matter is the **primary research**, i.e. try contact experts or insiders and try to interview them. **Secondary research** is analysis of data and information from scientific articles, publications, books, statistics, newspapers etc.

If a topic is new for you, the best and quickest solution may be:

Go from simple to complex sources

Often, **Wikipedia** articles provide a basic understanding and summary of terms, institutions etc. Not all Wikipedia articles are perfect, but they often provide further literature references and citations which will help you. If you start directly with a scientific article, you may not know or understand the theories used in the background and you may not fully understand the intentions of the authors.

Other sources may be *Google, Yahoo, Lycos, Metacrawler* or other search engines. If you limit your Google search to Acrobat portable data format (**pdf**) files and enter your topic as search word, there is a good chance to find presentations of the topic, because PowerPoint presentations are displayed in Google often as pdf files. You may try the same in *Google Scholar*, which provides academic articles.

Go from secondary to primary sources

If you have the chance to talk to somebody, do not waste time with questions where the answer is already known. Any interview should be focused on the things that cannot be found in literature, i.e. the better the interview is prepared, the more effective it will be.

Was your job already done by somebody else?
It is very likely that you are not the first one who has to do the analysis, but where can you find such analyses?

In US, a good (= for free, no registration, high quality) source is the report page of **Congressional Research Service** (CRS), you can enter your issue as a search request on http://opencrs.com/ to get reports. The reports have also abstracts with references to other reports.
In the European Union, the easiest way to find and understand a certain policy is the EU gateway http://europa.eu/
You can choose your preferred language and then you can retrieve the policy areas of interest under http://europa.eu/pol/index_en.htm
The websites provide an overview on the most relevant involved parties and issues and gives an overview about the existing laws and actions.

Other standard sources are the websites of your government, of the responsible ministry, of political parties and which is very useful, of the associations and interest groups. For example in Germany, you have about 12,000 associations for almost every possible topic under www.verbaende.com.
In contrast to former times, many actors want your attention and provide downloads and brochures for free which often contain the most important issues.

Think tanks are institutions that do professional policy analysis. A website of many think tanks in the European Union (for free, no registration) is available e.g. on http://www.eu.thinktankdirectory.org/,
for Germany on http://www.thinktankdirectory.org/,
in the US e.g. on http://www.hks.harvard.edu/library/research/guides/think-tanks-directory.htm.

Read the websites of your opponents: This may sound strange, but to be 100% sure that you covered all aspects of a matter, it may be useful to visit the websites your opponents, even if they are your worst enemies. Often, they present weak points and critical issues while supporter websites tend to ignore them. A really good analysis has to present the main arguments *for and against* a matter. If you don't agree with an argument, you have to explain, why this is not correct.

2.2.3 Five Simple Questions

Five simple questions can be used to keep your analysis focused:

Question 1: What is the political issue/result?

Define the topic as precisely as possible to save time and resources. There are large and small policy areas, such as economic policy as large area and tax policy as small area. Sometimes, a topic is related to more than one area, this is called **cross-sectoral policy**, e.g. urban policy. Try to keep your area as small as possible. If you prefer a wider perspective, you may expand the analysis at a later stage.

Question 2: Which policy sector (policy area) is affected?

There is no official or fully accepted definition of a policy area, but it consists of elements that you have to identify for your topic.

In any case there has to be a **topic** that is under discussion (e.g. social or economic or security and so on…). Then, try to identify individuals or groups dealing with this matter, these are the **actors**. Relevant actors can be governmental (part of the state) or non-governmental (e.g. trade unions). The mode of action can be **government** (the issue managed by the state) or **governance**, i.e. involving non-governmental actors and actions.

There will be formal and informal (unwritten) rules, in Political Science known as **institutions**. There is often more than one level; you may have international agreements (treaties, organizations) and national law. In the European Union, European and national law can both exist for a certain sector => clarify which political/administrative level is responsible. In the EU, there are currently 32 policy sectors where the EU has the sole or shared responsibility.

Question 3: Who wants what from which actor?

When you have identified an actor, ask *what they want* and even more important *what they can*. Please note: sometimes they don't want to do anything and to keep the things as they are, these situations are called **non-decisions**.

There are four main causes/motives for a political action: **cost-benefit** calculations, **beliefs/values** and norms, making or changing of **rules** and **power** politics.

These four motives may appear as **motive mix**. A party may e.g. support a new law, because it safes money, but may also be fair from an ethical point of view. This new law may bring some new rules and of course, the law has to be successful, otherwise the party may loose the next elections.

You may also find other motives in literature, but the above mentioned motives are most frequently mentioned and discussed.

However, sometimes it is not clear that people can really control something. There are four different perspectives:

- **actor-based theories**: actors control and form the environment and society
- **functionalism**: constraints and requirements may lead to a kind of automatism in some situations
- **structuralism**: structural factors are most relevant (e.g. demographic structure of the population)
- **System theory**: there a many variants of system theory in literature. While **Talcott Parsons** analyzed the social actions system with his **AGIL scheme** (adaptation, goal attainment, integration and latent pattern maintenance as system functions), the theoretical focus of **Luhmann** was on the role of communication in the systems and subsystems and the functional differentiation of systems.

A typical analytical error is the use of **fictional actors**: 'Actors' are often oversimplified, e.g. as ,the state', ,the industry', where multiple actors and interests are behind these terms.

Question 4: Which problems and conflicts result?
For almost everything, you will find different opinions and views. For the analysis of disputes and debates it is essential to ask whether these differences cause real and **relevant** conflicts.

Try to avoid trivial answers like: 'opposition is against governing party' etc., try to find the specific conflicts.

What does relevance mean? Political parties/associations consist of many people, so you will ever have 'internal disputes'. These disputes are relevant if have a real influence on political decisions/actions/processes.

Another problem is the analysis of claims and concerns. There are many lobby organizations, who claim that they/their people are underprivileged/ underpaid/ignored by government etc. Before you consider this in your argumentation, **try to find evidence**. A pressure group will never state that they have enough money and are fully satisfied…

Question 5: Which solutions were already suggested or implemented?
A suggested solution was possibly discussed, implemented or rejected somewhere else. Try to check this and find out what happened.
Statistics and figures often give room for interpretation, but try to look on the general picture and not to focus too much on details.

2.2.4 Three analytical approaches
Three analytical approaches that can be used in parallel are:
Process analysis: e.g. the development of a new law (How?)
Causal analysis: what are the motives and rationales behind a political action (Why?)
Political advice: analysis of arguments and creation of new arguments (What can/should be done?).
These approaches are presented in the next section in detail.

2.3 Process Analyses

The understanding of political processes has completely changed in the 20th century, with a trend to more complex and differentiated views. There were four main phases of process analysis.

Phase I Hierarchical policy
In former times, it was common to believe that the state makes political decisions and actions on its own in a hierarchical manner, e.g. by orders of a king. But this was never entirely true, already in ancient times there were 'lobbyists', e.g. merchants who made suggestions to promote trade by an appropriate tax and customs policy.

Phase II Easton's input-conversion output model
A great step forward was Eastons input-conversion-output model. In detail, this model is complex, but simply spoken, **input** by pressure groups (demands and supports) is converted by the **policy making system** to **output** (decisions and

actions). There were discussions that the policy making system looked a bit like a black box or slot machine.

Phase III Policy-Cycle

A widely used very simple model is the policy cycle, i.e. the idea that the political process never ends and if you have made a decision, the next issues will come up soon. Many variants of this model and the terminology are known in literature, so the model below is only a simple variant.

Tab. 1 Policy Cycle

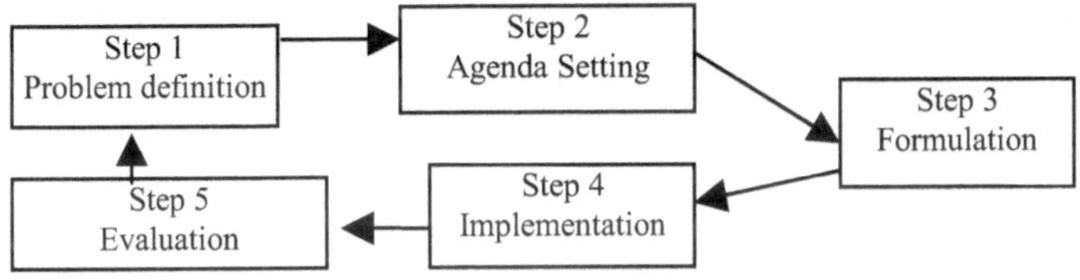

Problem definition:

There are urgent political issues, e.g. too many unemployed and poor people, but what is now the 'problem'? Is this a low qualification level of the people, a lack of social security systems, is there need to promote industry or investments or is the economy simply not competitive anymore? A clear problem definition is needed but already this can lead to conflicts, because the definition will influence the discussed solutions.

Agenda setting:

You need to put your problem on the political agenda, i.e. politicians need to take care of the problem. **Cobb** and **Ross** have raised various issues here:

An **internal agenda setting** is when issues will be handled on a technical/administrative level without further public discussion while an **external agenda setting** is initiated by the public or there is a relevant participation of the public. Topics may be escalated from the internal to the external level and may also diffuse to other levels, e.g. from a national to an international level.

Sometimes there are so-called **policy windows**; these are windows of opportunities where actors and the public become aware of a certain matter and you have suddenly the chance to change something, e.g. implementation of international alert systems after the Tsunami disaster in 2004.

Formulation:

The formulation of a possible solution may consider several options:

A widely accepted classification of political measures is based on the *Four systems of Policy, Politics and Choice* acc. to **Theodore Lowi**:

* regulative – by rules (law, guidance, regulations)
* distributive – giving money for a certain political issue
* redistributive – redistribute money from one group to another. Advantage: cost-effective, disadvantage: matter of conflicts
* social regulative – (**Salisbury/Heinz**): transfer of rights/responsibilities to non-governmental actors (such as **private governments**)

Other discussed political strategies are:

* persuasive policy –convince other people
* symbolic policy– influence other people with meaningful words, actions, symbols (e.g. flags, hymns).

There is no general rule which instrument has to be used in a certain situation. However, if you don't have money, regulative actions may save money and/or offload the costs to other actors. Redistribution will probably lead to conflicts with those groups who should give their money to others.

Transfer of responsibilities is often done in situations where technical issues have to be regulated; a good example is the regulation of technical norms by organizations like the International Standardization Organization ISO. These norms may not legally binding, but a producer will probably be liable if an accident happens and the norms were not considered.

Persuasion is typically used when you have not enough power to make a political action on your own.

Symbolic actions are sometimes interpreted as irrational and old-fashioned, but they are still very important. They can even cause conflicts, e.g. in the current conflict between Macedonia and Greece with regard to the political heritage of Alexander the Great.

In the **implementation phase**, the law or decision comes into force and **implementation deficits** may appear, i.e. the law or decision is insufficiently conducted. A reason may be that the surveillance needs too much personnel and nobody can control the rules. Or a violation of a law cannot be shown easily so violations are not punished. Or the law is too complex and the guidance for handling is missing or impracticable.

Implementation research has revealed a lot of analytical and practical problems:

- The resulted maybe unexpected or unintended (**unintended policy outcome**): e.g. as **free-rider phenomenon** when many people change their behavior to protect the environment, but a few do not. These few nevertheless may profit from clean air etc.

- Another discussed phenomenon is the **contingency**: two events that are not related occur at the same time, e.g. the growth of economy under a new government. It seems plausible to conclude that the new government is responsible for success of national economy, but is there really a relationship? Maybe long-term effects of laws released by the former government or the rise of the global economy or modernization of industry by their owners are the true reasons.

- An analytical error can be the so-called **ex-post attribution of sense** (Mayntz), i.e. people try to make things logic where no logic exists.

- Sometimes it is intended that nothing happens or changes, this is called **Non-decision**. Reasons can be e.g. blockades, sitting something out, lack of money or agreements.

- A critical issue is a **hidden agenda**, i.e. secret goals behind the facade. *Be careful:* without having at least some evidence, do not argue with a hidden agenda, otherwise your analysis may end in conspiracy theories.

- Sometimes you have **interactions between policy areas** which may be an obstacle for your policy, e.g. tensions between social welfare and economic policy.

Evaluation: Finally, it has to be checked whether a political measure was effective or not and what has to be done next. Sometimes the difference between an old and a new government is smaller than expected. Schmidt has formulated this problem with two *research questions: Do parties matter? Does politics matter?*

Often people ask: *Why don't we make big reforms instead of minor changes?*
An important finding is the **incrementalism problem**, the politics of small steps. Often the policy of today looks like the policy of yesterday, it seems to follow **policy pathways.** The main reasons and motives found in research are:

Caution

- **risk aversion**: big changes can also be big mistakes, it maybe wise to go ahead in smaller steps
- **competence-difference gap**: new challenges are often handled by established methods from past events which makes things more calculable and past experience can be utilized.

Dependencies

- **cross-sectoral interactions:** if taxes increases, tax payers may try to invest their money in other countries (or may bring their money to 'tax paradises' etc.)

Administrative problems

- **pre-planned budgets**: e.g. in research policy, you have long-term budgets and sudden revisions may damage the research projects
- **administrative structure:** new laws and procedures should somehow fit with the administrative routines and organizational structure, otherwise you have to pay the price (frictions, learning curve)
- **legal constraints:** e.g. constitution, laws, international treaties. In federal states, it may not be possible to offload administrative costs to the regional levels without their agreement

Tactical issues

- **positive and negative coordination**: you need to know what you would like to do if the others would not exist to create visions and ideas (**negative coordination**), but then you have to consider the expectations of other resorts to achieve a realistic approach (**positive coordination**)
- **need for compromises**: politics is a never-ending game and you may need the others in the future, so it may be dangerous to ignore or to press them
- **modification of laws** during political process: within ministries, in the cabinet, by lobbying etc.

Phase IV: Political action can be characterized as 'muddling through'
The concept of policy cycle suggests a systematic and stepwise procedure which is often not the case. Sometimes the cycle may even go backwards, e.g. a law may fail

or things may change during discussion and the entire problem needs to be redefined.

Often, politicians act under high pressure and without time to analyze and discuss things thoroughly. A model that reflects this is the **Garbage can model** of **Cohen, March** and **Olsen** where

* solutions (technologies), which look for applications (e.g. magnet train Transrapid)
* people/actors try to involve themselves
* problems that need to be resolved

meet together in an unorganized manner like the papers in a garbage can.

It is noteworthy that even routine decisions are typically not done automatically or even mathematically.

Nevertheless, some authors believe that this model reflects only parts of the political practice. Sometimes, you have strategies and long-term planning, e.g. in the European Union some regulations are discussed and prepared systematically over many years, e.g. the liberalization of the telecommunication sector where a lot of regulations were released within the framework of a liberalization concept since the 1990ies.

2.4 The Main Motives of Policy-Making

The 4 most frequently mentioned motives are
* cost-benefit-calculation (rational choice)
* values and beliefs
* making/changing/following/violating rules and
* power politics: controlling resources, people, territories and information.

These 4 motives are core elements of **paradigms**, i.e. a basic theoretical framework, simply spoken the general way of thinking.

2.4.1 Cost-Benefit-Calculation: Rational Choice Paradigm

The concept of **methodological individualism** holds the idea that social situations or collective actions are the sum of individual actions (and not more). The idea is, if you would remove all individuals from a society, there is no society anymore. Thus, society is the sum of individuals.

Social Scientists contradict, they argue that human beings are born into already existing societies and usually, not all people of a society die at the same time. Therefore, the history, traditions, and education given by a society may have relevant influence on individuals and society is more than the sum of its members.

The individuals are **rational actors**, i.e. they try to maximize benefit and to minimize costs in a certain situation. In Latin, this is the so-called **homo oeconomicus** i.e. the economically thinking and acting man.

Another frequently used concept is the **Utilitarianism (Latin usus = benefit)**: Utilitarianism is the idea that the worth of an action is determined by its contribution to overall utility. A situation where the overall welfare/utility cannot be increased any more is called '**Pareto efficient**'. Utilitarianism arguments may ignore the interests and rights of minorities and may lead to a politics that can be characterized as so-called '**dictatorship of the majority**'.

The concept is under discussion for other reasons as well. If an objective overall welfare/utility/happiness would really exist, a so-called **benevolent dictator** could implement this on behalf of the people and parties and different opinions would not be needed. However, the existence of different parties and opinions indicates that this objective maximum does not exist.

Moreover, are people really rational? People have emotions, make mistakes, are in error, misinterpret or oversee facts, they have a **bounded rationality** (Simon)[1].

A major problem of rational action in politics is the **difference between individual rationality** (what is good for me?) and **common rationality** (what is good for all of us?)

- High bonus payments are attractive for managers, but may damage the bank
- **NIMBY** (Not in my backyard)-Phenomenon: it is comfortable to have a short distance to airport, but who wants to live close to the airport?
- **free-rider problem**: others buy a new car to reduce air pollution, but also those who still drive their old ones also profit from the improved air
- **common goods**: overuse of common goods, such as extensive fishery in the oceans

---

[1] For example, in marketing it is clear that consumers are often not rational. **Searching costs** may be too high to find the cheapest good and they take, what they get in a short time. Often, consumers have a pre-selection of brands and products in their mind, **evoked set**.

- **negative externality**: A third party has to bear the costs of agreement between two other parties.

In conclusion, even full individual rationality *does not* guarantee good policy results.

The **principal-agent-theory** shows further problems. In large companies, not the owners (principal), but employed managers are doing the daily work as agents. However, these agents may have other interests than the owners. The ‚owners' may consist of thousands of shareholders who cannot control the much better informed board of managers. This phenomenon is also called **asymmetric information** and is an important reason why delegation may make your life not easier.….

An important application of the rational choice paradigm is the **Economic Theory of Democracy of Anthony Downs**, who analyzed voters as benefit-maximizing and cost-minimizing people. For the political party, the aim must be to achieve 50%+1 vote, this voter is the **median voter**. A practical consequence is that parties who want to achieve the majority often tend to the middle of the political spectrum. However, this may lead to loss of the political profile and left- and right-wing parties may take over the margins then, so this is a balancing act. However, often voters have emotional and traditional reasons to vote for a certain party and also milieus (social environments) may influence the voting.

Other applications related to rational decision making are analyzed by the **Game theory**.

Prisoner's dilemma

Two persons are imprisoned, but the police have not enough evidence to punish them appropriately. If both prisoners do not cooperate, they may only be punished for a short time, e.g. 2 years. If one cooperates and betrays the other one, he may get reduced punishment (e.g. one year) and the other gets 9 years. If both blame each other, they may get 7 years, because then the cooperation was not really needed. The problem is now: *Should I cooperate or not?* Can I trust the other one who has a strong incentive to betray me in this special situation?

Tab. 2 Prisoner's Dilemma

	Prisoner B Stays Silent	**Prisoner B Betrays**
Prisoner A Stays Silent	Each serves 2 years	Prisoner A: 9 years Prisoner B: 1 year
Prisoner A Betrays	Prisoner A: 1 year Prisoner B: 9 years	Each serves 7 years

In political practice, this is relevant for **cartels**, but also for terrorist groups and criminal groups, where states try to break up these groups by a leniency program. Criminals try to counteract by extreme punishments for those who talk …

Chicken Game

Two people drive at each other on a narrow road. The first to swerve loses faces, because the observers may believe that he is afraid (chicken-hearted) and not tough enough. If neither swerves, they will collide and maybe dead afterwards.

In political practice, the chicken game reflects the problems of escalating conflicts. If somebody threats and the other one does not react, you are the chicken, if you don't or can't make your threat to come true. On the other hand, each party needs to know the exit-options in an escalating conflict, otherwise they pass the point of no return and you have to attack the other side. During the Cold war, it was essential to know when a critical point was reached; otherwise an escalation could have resulted in a nuclear war.

Tit for tat strategy: this is <u>not</u> the strategy of revenge and retaliation, but means: when the other one cooperates, you should cooperate, too, even when the other one is usually your opponent. But if the other one does not cooperate anymore, you should stop your cooperation, too, otherwise you loose your credibility. An ongoing cooperation between former enemies may be a way to build trust between the acting parties. A good example is the exchange of captured spies between US und Russia during the Cold War which worked well for many years.

Battle of the sexes: in this situation somebody has to abstain from something. The typical example is when a man and a woman want to do something together, but the man would like to go to a sports event while the women would like to go to the theater. At the end, someone has to give up here or there is no common activity. Sometimes it may make sense to act so, if you can expect that the other persons will give you something at another time point, too. This is also called **shadow of the future**, i.e. you never know what the future brings and the other one may need you then.

Veto-player: this is an actor who has to accept something, because otherwise a decision cannot be made. The power of veto may be due to legal or on practical reasons and one can try **bargaining** or **logrolling** ('you vote this time for me, next time I vote for you') or to convince the veto player by **arguing**.

In political practice, actors are often communicating in formal or informal **networks** (sometimes issue-specific) that allow early communication and avoid conflicts in latter stages of the political process.

2.4.2 Values, Traditions and Norms

2.4.2.1 Introduction

Human beings grow up in already existing societies and during education and **socialization**, they learn about the values, norms and traditions of their society. However, this influences their point of view.

A good example are poor people: some people think they are often not really willing to work and therefore responsible for their situation while others are convinced that they are often victims e.g. of economic crises or unfair work relations. Depending on your opinion, you will handle his problem differently, e.g. with regard to amount and duration of social welfare in case of unemployment.

This is the **social construction of reality**, i.e. the way how you interpret facts is influenced by your individual and social background.

There may even be no objective truth for some political problems and then you have to follow your own beliefs. In the Roman Empire, it was discussed for several hundreds of years whether poor people in Rome should be supported by cheap food or not.

Economic practice is **socially embedded**, because business is part of social practice, economy is not outside society. An example is that charging of interests for credits may be prohibited by religion.

Social practice has also influence on technical design. We still write *cc:* in our emails, but a *carbon copy* (this is what cc: means) is not existing anymore and based on typewriters and also we have still QWERTY as first letters on our computers (which was historically used to avoid deadlocks during typing).

2.4.2.2 Values and Beliefs

Often you can distinguish between **deep core beliefs**, these are principles that you will follow or defend under any circumstances, but you can also have **policy core beliefs**, i.e. things that you support in a certain situation. People with common beliefs may form **advocacy coalitions** (model of **Sabatier**).

Shared values and beliefs may result in the formation of political parties, programs or even ideologies that try to explain how the world is and how *it should be* (target state).

2.4.2.3 Political Concepts and Ideologies

The most common political concepts are presented shortly below.

For **liberalism** many variants are known, but the core idea is the free and self-responsible individual. **Adam Smith** discussed the **laissez-faire state** that should provide a legal framework, but should not do interventions into private affairs. The free market is a preferable way to solve problems (by the interaction of supply and demand), a mode that was called **invisible hand**.

Hayek argued that market corrections will result in a bias that requires 'corrections of corrections' and so on.... Others argued that a free market would destroy itself, because large companies will try to eliminate competition in the long run (monopoly paradox).

Conservatives (Latin: conservare: to keep, maintain) try to keep and maintain existing structures and values. With this broad definition, also left-wing parties can be conservative, e.g. in the former Soviet Union where the leaders tried to keep the existing order. In many countries, e.g. Germany, conservatives have also religious roots and try to keep e.g. Christian values relevant for political practice.

The **Green** parties were founded as a reaction to increasing environmental problems in the late 1970ies. At the beginning, they acted as grassroots movement and tried to achieve their goals outside parliament, but meanwhile Green parties are established in several European parliaments.

Marxism is a materialistic philosophy which was founded by **Karl Marx**. His friend and supporter **Friedrich Engels** helped to formulate the theories of Marx in a more understandable and practicable manner which is the reason why Engels is very important for Marxism, but why no ‚Engelsianism' exists. The core issue was the conflict between the owners of the resources (the capitalists) and those who have to work for them, the workers and farmers as Proletarians (**class conflict**). Marx expected that the unfair working and ownership relationships with exploitation and alienation would lead to a revolution. The resulting socialistic society would be based on solidarity and would finally develop to **communism** without private ownership. Instead, everything would be owned then by the society as a whole.

The **social democrats** which competed with Marxism since the 1860ies argued, that the situation of workers and farmers should be improved stepwise (**evolutionary**) within the existing system and not by a revolution. Marxists criticized this position as '**revisionism**' and argued that this would stabilize capitalism.

The **Leninism** was created by **Lenin** who also founded the Soviet Union. He argued that the revolution needs to coordinated by a **cadre party** which is dominated by political elite groups of activists. His fraction within the Russian Social Democratic Party was called **Bolsheviki** which led to the term **Bolshevism**.
In the last phase of his government, Lenin initiated some market-oriented economic reforms. These were completely cancelled by his successor **Stalin** who returned to a planned economy with fixed prices and imprisoned and eliminated millions of real or suspected opponents. There were also ideological disputes: he promoted the revolution in one country while **Trotsky** suggested the international revolution export. Moreover, Stalin promoted the industrial development as first priority instead of agriculture. The term **Stalinism** is now mainly used to describe the practices and not the ideology.
After the end of the cold war, it was discussed whether communism has come to end, what the difference between socialism and communism is and there are also a lot of different 'socialisms'.
Usually, modern 'socialist' states have a policy where the state explicitly preserves the right to influence and control economy, if needed, while 'capitalist' states try to

avoid this, if possible. Socialism does not necessarily mean a planned economy anymore, but sometimes fixed prices for important goods are still used.

There is a discussion in Western media whether China is a 'capitalist' state now. While the daily business as microeconomic level changed significantly since the communist era, the state has still relevant control over economy on a macroeconomic level. This allowed China to manage the financial crisis e.g. by instructing the banking system to continue with credits so from a theoretical point of view this seems to be a mix of socialist and capitalist elements.

China with more than 1 billion people is still ruled by a Communist party. However, there were important modifications of the Communist theory. The most important one is the concept of **the three representations** (sange daibiao) that means that the party should represent in addition to farmers, workers and soldiers also progressive forces in economy and culture and thus the broad majority of Chinese people, i.e. to stop the class conflict. The new ideal of **harmonic society** refers to classic Confucian concepts, i.e. also religious people and churches may be acceptable, if they don't act against the government. There are ongoing disputes with Western states and NGOs who both criticize the Chinese government as too rigid with regard to minorities and opponents, but Chinese government does not agree and rejects this as an inappropriate intervention into internal affairs.

Fascism (derived from *fasci di combattimento*, the 'fighting groups') was created by the socialist Italian politician Mussolini as reaction to the disappointing first World War. He proposed a strong state with harmony, i.e. no class conflicts. This model was taken over by other countries, in particular Germany. Typical for fascist states were e.g. structures with employers and employees in the same organization. Internally, the existence of strong leader was the guiding principle. The nation was more than society, it was seen as community. Those groups who did not fit in this concept were entirely excluded from society, e.g. the Jews, homosexuals, communists and other groups and millions of them were imprisoned and killed.

After Word War II, was a theoretical dispute whether communism and fascism is practically the same due to the intended total control of the individuals (**totalitarian** states) or if there is a major difference due to the different ideology (fascism as last try to maintain capitalist structures while communism wants to destroy them; **fascism theory**). Meanwhile, most authors accept that there are ideological differences and some similar organizations (e.g. State Youth organizations) at the same time. While communism claims to be scientific (scientific Marxism), fascist parties often argue with beliefs and myths. While classes are a core element of communism, fascism argues with nations and races.

A new topic is **Islamism,** the idea to promote Islamic belief, traditions and values in societies. There is a dispute with regard to the causes. One position is that social conflicts are the main reason for the rise of political-religious movements (like for the Christian movements of the medieval age). These movements often emphasize topics like justice and community.

The suggestion is to reduce social disparity in the concerned countries. Another position argues that these movements are often not controlled by or based on poor people, but are managed by rich and educated people (political elites) and are also used as instrument in power politics. Despite this dispute, both positions emphasize that this should not be mixed up with terrorism which is only made by a few radical people.

Whatever is true, there is a global comeback of religious movements, also many Christian churches report increasing memberships. Also, it is observed in some states, that the younger people are even more religious than the older ones and/or that religion is a part of the traditional way of life and therefore a relevant part of the national identity.

The role of culture

There are many definitions of the term 'culture'. According to the widest definition, culture is the opposite of nature, i.e. the sum of all man-made things. A strict definition limits culture to fine arts and classics and all things of 'real' value, but there is no agreement what is covered by that. In the 20th century, comics were often called "trash"; meanwhile some of them achieve high prices and are well-respected.

Luhmann suggested a moderate definition: *"culture is observed society"*. This definition means that culture is not that we have homes, cars, go to work, have music and dancing, but is *how* we live, *how* we work, *how* our music and dancing looks like.

There are many other definitions, but the simple interpretation of culture as way of living may be useful for Political Science.

Political culture can be seen as the general orientation of the citizens of a nation toward politics, which has relevant influence on their perceptions of political legitimacy. For example, Germans often do not like job changes of people between policy, science and economy. This is interpreted as mix-up of spheres that may be a source of hidden agendas, e.g. a politician who becomes a professor may not be fair and objective or a manager joining a political party may act as a lobbyist for his former company. In USA, there is much more exchange between political, economic and scientific sphere and it is argued that this brings new ideas and perspectives and prevents isolation of the spheres from each other.

Another perspective is Huntington's **Clash of Cultures** who believed that the future world will be a fight between Western, Asian and Islamic values. This was criticized by some authors as oversimplification and caused misleading interpretations, such as 'real democracy is only possible in a Western culture' which is not the case. However, his theory is still a matter of discussion.

2.4.3 Power Politics

Power is a matter not only in foreign policy, but also in internal affairs and even in personal relationships. However, the main focus of political theories of power (e.g. to explain globalization, commodities, peacekeeping etc.) is foreign policy and international relations.

Max Weber defined power *as the chance that an individual in a social relationship can achieve his or her own will even against the resistance of others*. This is the classical definition of power.

Mao Zedong defined power as a matter of force: *Political power grows out of the barrel of guns.*

In the management theory power is defined with irony as: *If you have power, you don't need to learn from your mistakes anymore.* Power is different from influence, which can be based on threats, incentives, and persuasion or by example. Power is also dependent on the ability to adapt the methods and instruments to changing situations.

In this area, the theories of **neo-realism** (focusing on power), the **neo-institutionalism** (focus on rules), **neo-functionalism** (focus on requirements and constraints)[2] and the **neo-Marxism** compete with each other.

Usually, the prefix **neo-** indicates modification of more older, more rigid theoretical approaches. While the original theories usually claim to provide very far-reaching explanations ("hypothesis z is true"), the modified theories accept restrictions for their theoretical scope (for example "if the conditions x and y apply, then z is true").

Realism: foreign policy is focused on gaining and maintaining power. Power is a **zero-sum game**, i.e. if someone is more powerful, the others have less power. Therefore, there may be military alliances, but the international system is not really stable. You cannot relay on international organizations, at the end you have to rely on yourself.

Neorealism: international agreements and arrangements are possible, but only under the **shadow of hierarchy**, i.e. somebody who can enforce an agreement in case of disagreement between the members of an organization. In Greek, this leading power was called **Hegemon**. At the end of the day, international organizations are only derivates, i.e. instruments of the national states who have the real power in the background. The increasing number of international organizations cannot be interpreted voluntary takeover of best practices and structures (**isomorphism**), but only as **emulation**, i.e. as taking over some structures without supporting the idea of power sharing. If a powerful state would not accept these organizations anymore, then they would collapse.

Neorealists prefer **Unilateralism**, i.e. acting alone, because others may confuse or disturb your political action. If you act in international organizations, you may be involved in issues and conflicts that are not useful or relevant for you. Moreover, the role of **non-governmental organizations (NGOs)** is criticized, because they would have only a selective view on things and involve themselves without democratic legitimacy. The NGOs argue that they fill gaps in the international

---

[2] Functionalism is in particular relevant for the European Union. However, there is no automatism that forces states to build up a European state. In neo-functionalism, a **spill-over effect** is discussed, where integration in one policy sectors will increase pressure on other sectors.

political system, because they take care for problems that governments are not willing or able to solve such as torture, corruption or protection of species.

Neo-Institutionalism: The old institutionalism discussed a determinative effect of formal institutions. The current neo-institutionalism also considers **informal** institutions and the influence on actors which is not seen anymore as determinative.

An important theory is the **complex interdependence (Keohane/Nye)** which is characterized by the use of multiple channels of action between societies in international relations relations, the absence of a hierarchy of issues with changing agendas and linkages and the decline in the use of military force and coercive power in international relations. Some authors describe this as **Embedded Liberalism**, i.e. markets are embedded in a regulative environment.

Neo-Marxist theories analyze how capitalism was able to maintain its dominant position, because in classic Marxism the collapse of capitalism was expected and various issues are discussed.

Social welfare systems help to stabilize the societies internally and to reduce conflicts between the classes. Another factor is the so-called **fordism** with mass production which allows producing cheap products for mass consumption. This is even more even effective if wages are low, but not too low so that the workers can buy the products. Please note that fordism has different meanings in literature, so this was presented as an example.

On an international level, **global constitutionalism** is an important matter. This means global legal frameworks for certain areas. Neo-Marxists criticize that capitalism and in particular US-law are dominant in such frameworks.

Today, power means control over people, territories, resources and information and the international term for these matters is **geopolitics**. In the so-called **Great Game** states try to control energy sources and/or their transport routes, e.g. by treaties, influence on governments of neighbor states etc. They try to bypass states via sea pipelines (North Stream pipeline through the Baltic Sea) or by **Off-shoring**, e.g. in Western Africa where companies exploit the oil by platforms which are far away from regional conflicts and they simply send the license fees to the local government (whoever this is).

In **dependencia theories** developing countries are seen as dependent from industrial countries based on unfair price relations (**terms of trade**), so the developing countries stay poor. A fair trade is needed here. On the other hand, the **modernization theory** says that old-fashioned traditions and structures in developing countries are the main reasons for the problems of these regions and it is argued that the political leaders of these countries have to change their mind.

Meanwhile ecologic approaches where limited resources control politicians and not vice versa are under discussion. Jered Diamond presented in his book **Collapse** that not simply the growth of mankind, but the increasing wealth will lead to collapse of the environmental system. As a consequence, Western countries need to change their way a life to a more sustainable manner. Some authors believe that there is another message between the lines: If the Western countries want to keep their way of life, they need to keep to others down and poor. This issue is e.g. discussed in more detail by Gabor Steingart in his book **World war about welfare**.
This discussion may explain why the states are not able or willing to agree upon an enforceable reduction of carbon dioxide despite climate change and melting of the pole caps.

In international relationships, the **End of the Nation State** is discussed. The nation state seems to be more and more irrelevant or overstretched in the age of globalization and international organizations. However, it this true? The last two decades have seen a lot of new nation states such as in former Yugoslavia, in the former Soviet Union, Eritrea, and Eastern Timor, the split of Abkhazia and South Ossetia from Georgia and in 2011 Sudan may be split up into two states. There are also centrifugal movements in Spain and UK.

2.4.4 Institutionalism
Institutions[3] can be interpreted as historically grown, e.g. as traditions, as norms, as rules and they can also have integrative functions as framework.
The **Actor-Centered Institutionalism** in Policy Research (**Mayntz/Scharpf**) discusses that political decisions are the results of interactions between actors and their institutional framework.

---

[3] When being more strict, this is Neo-Institutionalism, but usually people talk only about ‚institutionalism'.

For politics, it is relevant who makes the rules and how they are designed, because they may be of disadvantage for third parties. The USA as a leading economic power often tries to convince the European Union to take over the American legal framework. Even if this maybe advantageous for both sides to reduce frictions and legal uncertainties, Europeans have to bear additional adaptation and transaction costs, e.g. for European companies registered at US stock exchanges when the US **Sarbanes-Oxley Act** was implemented with a lot of consequences for accounting practices. Sometimes, the USA has the same problem, e.g. with the European data protection agreement **safe harbor**, which was finally accepted by several large US companies. The neo-institutionalism was in particular discussed during the era of liberalization and globalization in the 1980ies and 1990ies.

2.4.5 Political Advice

The discussion whether scientists should give political advice was called the **argumentative turn**; policy analysis should not only analyze arguments, but should also be used for providing new arguments (political advice).

There are many possibilities for advice, but a frequently used method is the **scenario technique**; one example out of many is given below.

Scenario-method e.g. UK Strategic trends 2007-2036
The British Ministry of Defense has initiated a study with scenarios for the next three decades.

Based on available information, unlikely to probable future developments are mentioned (page xii, xiv). Main hypothesis: It is not true, that it is not possible to predict future at least with a certain probability, because future is based on events that happened in the past.

The scope of security is expanded to all factors that influence the stability of a society. A stable society is essential for a secure society. This is different from the established security definition, where a state is secure, if the responsible authorities have enough rights, money and personnel to fight against threats.

Two results (out of many) were e.g.

• there may be increasing tensions between the old and young generation in particular due to the burden of care. The elderly may have safe and higher pensions while the young may suffer from insecure jobs and low wages.

- pauperizing societies may have stronger emphasis on values, norms and traditions to keep the society stable.

3. Modern Governance and Control

3.1 Introduction

In ancient times, the state was seen as the great thinker and disposer and therefore, the state gave the orders in a hierarchical manner (vertical = top-down). During the prosperity of Western countries in the 1960ies and 1970ies, the state often acted as **active state** and the idea was that the state does all things the market cannot provide (**market failure**). However, after the oil crises of 1973/74 and 1980/1981, prosperity has gone and the budgets were limited. This led to the concept of the **lean state** with privatization of services wherever possible. Moreover, the state should act more economically and profit-oriented to be more efficient. The idea was now that the market should solve the problems instead of the state, wherever possible (**state failure**).

The re-orientation to market was supported by the **Laffer curve** that showed that the tax level of the state can also be too high, i.e. it can stall the economy. In that case, reduced taxes could stimulate economy so that the total tax income would be even higher than before.

Milton Friedman and other representatives of the so-called **Chicago School** argued that the state should reduce its activities to areas where the state is really needed and that state is often active in economic sectors where the state is not needed and not efficient. Also, the fight against inflation was emphasized as a stable monetary value will bring trust and reliability to economic relations (**monetarism**). This policy requires a stop of **deficit spending** as it was suggested by the theories of **John Maynard Keynes**. Keynes recommended spending money to stimulate economy during crises, because during Great Depression this was not done and this decision had a negative impact on global economy in the 1930ies. Keynes argued that the state has to save money in better times to pay back the debts, but in practice, this part of this theory was often not considered. However, the stop of deficit spending is often linked with cut-off of social services. Unfortunately, Keynes' theories gave much room for interpretations and there are various '**Keynesianisms**'.

The re-orientation to market and the emphasis on monetary stability was soon labeled as **neo-liberalism**, but please note that this term also has many different meanings in detail in literature. If you discuss neo-liberalism with others, please make sure that the others have the same understanding of this or try to clarify the differences.

But meanwhile, Western states are under increasing pressure, e.g. by new competitors (such as Brazil, Russia, India and China BRIC) and by demographic problems, so the discussion went on to the diagnosis of a **combined state and market failure**. As a solution, the state should act as an **activating state**, this includes mobilization of organizations of the **third sector** (third sector = neither market nor state, such as NGOs, religious communities, voluntarism etc.) and their increased participation in political processes. Also, the term **civil society** is used to describe all activities outside state and market. However, there are varying definitions of this term, so other understandings may also be found in literature.

For the involvement of non-governmental organizations and their equal participation in political processes the term **governance (the way of governing)** is increasingly used. The term governance has again a lot of different meanings in literature. However, it often used to describe modes of cooperation, where all actors are on the same level (**horizontal or non-hierarchical cooperation**) and many authors use this also for the participation of non-governmental organizations in political decisions.

Governance is discussed as a possible way to manage the increasing complexity and amount of problems. This does not necessarily mean less state, but more involvement of citizens in civil society.

3.2 The Role of the State

There are many theories and perspectives what the state is or should be the most relevant are presented in the table below:

Tab. 3 The Role of the State

state as	theory	
actor	Political Science	in 20th century, the state was often seen as objective actor in contrast to selfish parties. The idea of an objective state was often combined with negative views on democracy
arena	pluralism	state is an arena for different actors who follow their own interests and who try to achieve their own goals
instrument	Marxism	state is instrument of the ruling class
	Elite theory	state is instrument of an elite e.g. old established families
functionalism	Parsons system theory	state is the result of functional requirements
	Luhmann's system theory	state is system with subsystems
structure	Political Science	state as structure of relations, allocations
	Administrative Sciences	state as legal framework
	History	state as a result of historical processes
economic institution	Transaction cost-theory	state ensures efficient transactions between its members
sociologic approach	Colemans ,bath tub'	Problems of the society appear as macro phenomenon, then individuals perceive them and react as individuals on the micro-level, the sum of these reactions has an aggregated effect on the society again

3.3 State and Market

Often, we talk about the 'Western' states. There are shared values, e.g. democracy and human rights (but is true for many Non-Western states as well), but there are a lot of structural differences between the states. The differences between political systems are discussed in **comparative government research** while the economic differences are discussed in the **Varieties of Capitalism** theory.

3.3.1 Comparative Government Research

Usually, a state has a leadership, a government with a Cabinet (the body of ministers), and a parliament which has the power of legislation.

The second element is the administration which implements the law and has the power of execution.

Then there is a legal system with (ideally independent) judges who are organized in courts (higher and normal courts as well as specialized courts).

Ideally, there is no overlap between these elements; this is called **separation of powers.** Sometimes, media and television are called the **'fourth power'** due to their influence.

Main differences between states are:

The **political leadership** may be done by a prime minister or a president. Sometimes you have both, then the prime minister is the political leader while the president (or in some states the monarchy) represents the state as a whole. Sometimes, ministers can be also members of parliament at the same time while some countries do not allow this.

The **Parliament** may consist of one or two chambers (e.g. senate and congress in US, House of Commons and House of Lords in UK, Bundestag and Bundesrat in Germany). This is done to achieve balance of power between groups or between administrative levels (e.g. state and regions).

States may differ with regard to the role of **members of parliament**, senators in US may vote more independently while e.g. in Germany a very high parliamentary party discipline is expected.

Political parties: the USA is dominated by two large political parties while e.g. in France political parties were relatively unstable after World War II. In France, the mayors of large towns play an important role and having such a position increases the chance for a future presidency.

Voting systems/elections: some states use **majority voting** for elections, i.e. those who get the most votes in a region get all parliaments seats there, while other countries use a **proportional system**, e.g. if a party gets 43%, 43% of parliament seats will be assigned to this party. Some countries use **barring clauses** to avoid too many small parties, other countries believe that this is not democratic, but then this may result in multi-party parliaments and governments.

Political culture: Some countries usually have a one party-government, while other countries usually have coalitions or even minority governments. Sometimes, a consensus democracy is exercised (**Lehmbruch/Lijphardt**): This is typical for states where ethnic, religious, or ideological tensions to not allow stable majority of one party (The Netherlands 'Versäulung', Austria 'Proporz-system', Lebanon 'confessional's Parliament').

Federalism or centralism: strong federalism is typically observed in states that were unified on a voluntary basis, but where people did not want to have strong central government (USA, Canada, Australia and in the EU that is formally not a state).

3.3.2 Varieties of Capitalism VoC

According to **Hall** and **Soskice**, not only the state, but also the market can differ between states, this is addressed in the theory of Varieties of Capitalism VOC.

There are two main types, the Anglo-Saxon **Liberal Market Economy LME** and the Central European **Coordinated Market Economy CME**. While the LME is the classical market economy, the CME is historically based on special structures such as the so-called **corporatism**.

Tab. 4 Varieties of Capitalism

Model	**Coordinated market economy CME** Continental Europe e.g. Germany	**Liberal market economy LME** 'Anglo-Saxon type'
Decision making in companies	Committee based, so-called **dualistic system** with a supervisory board (Aufsichtsrat) strictly separated from executive board (Vorstand)	**Monistic structure**, President and CEO can be one person, often strong leadership
Cooperation	State and associations promote networks and try to agree on norms	More project-related cooperation between companies. They set standards and try to enforce them
General strategy	Stakeholder value (try to find agreements with relevant groups, also political and pressure groups, if possible)	Shareholder value (try to maximize value of stocks and dividends)
Investments	Credits given mainly by banks => as a consequence, banks tend to have shares of those companies to which them gave the credits	Stock exchange, bond emission, venture capital, private equity
Employees	Have strong associations/trade unions which often agree with employers associations on tariffs	Individual contracts
Participation in decision making	Yes, to some extent	no

Professional Education	Often in companies (in Germany dual system of school plus practice in companies) Tendency to specialized education	Outside the companies, more general education
Labor market	Regulated High level dismissal protection, but therefore more rigid and inflexible markets	'Hire and fire', but more flexible markets

The corporatism theory

Pluralism holds that political power in society is distributed among a wide number of groups. Moreover, there are many conflicting actors and groups and the state is the arena of these conflicts. However, this was not interpreted as a negative event; the theory accepts multiple interests and conflicts as a natural part of political process, i.e. discussions and disputes are normal while consensus is an exception. An **open society** with critical discussions is the best way to handle things because this gives the chance to detect and correct mistakes and false developments as early as possible (**Karl Poppers** concept of **piecemeal engineering**).

But already in the **theory of political parties** there were concerns that political parties may take the state as hostage and use it only for their interests and to give good jobs and other benefits to their people. On the other hand, no party has never-ending power in a democratic system, so there is still room for revisions.

The **corporatism theory** argued that this is an incomplete understanding of the society. Associations do not only act as lobbies, but also have stabilizing and supportive functions. They e.g. set internal standards, they bundle and form interests, they make communication easier, because the state has somebody to talk to etc. For example, in the 19th century, associations of craftsmen had double functions in Germany. On one hand, they were allowed to control their branch as official representatives and were allowed to set educational and quality standards etc. On the other hand, the state expected that they follow the expectations and laws of the state and help to enforce it in their branch. This was the starting point of the **CME**.

However, associations have a **Janus-faced role**[4]: they have to represent their members; on the other hand they have to be credible partners in political dialogue. This may explain, why the members of an association or party are often more radical and demanding than their leaders. Giving responsibility to non-governmental organizations, e.g. for quality control of cars like in Germany, leads to **private governments (Streeck/Schmitter)**, because these organizations can act on behalf of the state (for example to shut down your car if this defect). However, the state acts as a **shadow of hierarchy** in the background to avoid that these organizations get out of control (**Voelzkow**).

Some authors also discuss a ‚**Roman type' of capitalism** in particular in Catholic Southern European states where old and established families and family networks are important for all relevant levels of the economy. As politician, you have to find an agreement with these families if you really want to change something. However, strong families as owners of large companies also exist in CMEs and LMEs.

However, all three types are only ideal typologies; usually one can find elements of all economy types in each country, but with a different element mix.

There are also **different types of social welfare systems**:

In social welfare, there are also two main variants: **insurance model** based on payments for the insured members based on their salaries (Bismarck model) and the **Beveridge model**, where payments are based on taxes.

Gosta Esping-Andersen has proposed three models of welfare state: a **conservative model** with a low level of private elements; a **social democratic model** with redistribution and a high level of social welfare and a **liberal model** which is based on market mechanism and with a focus on self-responsibility.

The **National systems of Innovation (NSI)-theory** shows that in Research and Development (R&D) policy LME states tend to prefer technologies that are in late stage of development and have good chances to be marketed, while CME states are preferably funding platform technologies, e.g. the CME state Germany is leading in

---

[4] The Janus temple in the ancient Rome showed a statue called Janus with tow faces, one for peace, one for war , which is called janus-faced.

the biochip platform technology for genetic analysis while the Anglo-Saxon LME states dominate the research of pharmaceutical biotech medication.

3.4 Debate about Governance

3.4.1 Coase' Understanding of Governance

Coase wrote a book **The nature of the firm** 1937 where he asks, why and under what conditions should we expect firms to emerge? The reason are **transaction costs**, these are e.g. administrative costs for market use (e.g. a fee you have to pay to your ban k for a money transaction). Transactions costs can sometimes not be avoided, because your bank has real costs when they transfer your money. In theory, everything that is done in a company could be done by individuals also, but the higher the transaction costs are, the more effective a permanent structure, the company, will be.

This is also true for political issues. For formulation and enforcement of interests it makes sense to have political parties, associations and other actors and of course, the state.

However, it was asked whether you really need a large organization, because this may result in long communication ways, organizational slack etc. Why not outsourcing everything based on contracts? This is difficult due to various problems:

- **bounded rationality:** people are not fully rational, they make mistakes etc.
- **opportunistic behavior:** this can appear as incomplete or biased dissemination of information. **Ex ante-treaties** that try to regulate everything in advance are not possible, as nobody can predict the future. Therefore, the **ex post-analysis** of treaties is important.
- **Property rights**: jurisdiction also costs time and money, i.e. you cannot get your right for free. Therefore, a clear definition of **property rights** can reduce the transaction costs (**Property rights theory**).

These matters are discussed in detail in the **Transaction Cost Economics** and the **New Institutional Economics** that was in particular elaborated by **Oliver Williamson**. There, the governance structure is defined as *the institutional matrix within which transactions are negotiated* (Williamson).

40

3.4.2 Governance Under Discussion

However, there are lots of classical theories with their own perspective on these matters.

Mancur Olson assumed in his publication **Logic of Collective Action** that rational individuals are only joining a group if they have clear incentive such as a benefit reserved strictly for group members. However, in theories of civil society it is expected that people dedicate themselves to the community without such an incentive, so who will do the grassroots work? The situation is different for interest groups where the benefit for members is clear as in trade unions or lobbies.

However, **Coleman** uses the term **social capital** to describe resources which can be mobilized to build up institutions such as aid organizations. People are not only selfish, many like to work for something that is good, so these people invest time and money into activities of the civil society.

Salisbury uses the concept of the **political entrepreneur** to describe an actor who seeks to gain certain political and social benefits in return for providing the common goods. Those persons, e.g. founders of a new NGO, are willing to take over the grassroots work and the difficult start phase where the risk-benefit ratio is uncertain.

Tullocks by-product theory of revolution argues that changes in society are typically a by-product of individual activities, because social change means also individual risk. Many people are only supporting changes if the expected individual risk is low.

However, **Clark and Willson** show that during the life cycle of an organization things may change. At the beginning, people are often enthusiastic and motivated. If the organization grows, you need more formalized communication. If organizational change is not handled carefully, an anonymous and bureaucratic structure results.

If this happens, the time for **rent-seeking (Tullock-Krüger)** has come, i.e. members are looking for their own profit. A related theory is the **theory of aging democracy,** where more and more layers of organizations and interests lead to the **carro completo (the boat is full)-syndrome,** i.e. there is no chance for new ideas or new people and old-boys networks have everything under control.

Lehmbruch and **Czada** contradict, because people have **overlapping memberships** (e.g. in a political party and a trade union) and there are **cross-**

pressures between competing organizations that prevent democracy from encrustation. **Willems** argues that free-riders can be controlled by tit-for-tat strategies, i.e. if you only act selfish, the organization will not take care for your interests anymore.

Governance concepts are often optimistic with regard to bureaucracy. There, public administrations can act in a flexible and cooperative manner with others. There are doubts in classic theory:

Niskanens theory of bureaucracy
The administration tries to maximize budgets, but it is difficult to define the products of a public administration. Moreover, the situation is often not transparent enough and administrations may produce no profit. The administrative monopoly may result in too much overhead (slack).
Administration have often more specialist information then the politicians who are responsible and as politicians often don't like to fight against the 'machine', they are not really motivated to do massive cut-offs.

Downs model of bureaucracy
Main actor is the head of the administration. Political entrepreneurs build up new administrations, if there is an opportunity to do so, climbers expand the bureaucracy, and then stagnation starts. To control the bureaucrats, you need more bureaucrats..... **Simon** argues that budget maximization is not really the goal, because bounded rationality does not allow defining such a maximum. The people tend more to do **satisfycing behavior**, i.e. not maximizing money, but less stress, more people, larger offices, shorter working times can also be attractive.

3.4.3 Governance and Theory of Democracy
The government theory suggests involving non-governmental organizations (NGOs) into political action. But where is the democratic legitimacy for them? Does this indicate a failure of democracy?
There are a lot of aspects under discussion. While **Rousseau** preferred a direct democracy of people by imperative mandates and plebiscites, others like **Montesquieu** suggested a representative (indirect) democracy where elected members of parliament decide. Representative democracies allow the involvement

of experts in policy making. Please note that Rousseau suggested the direct model only for small communities and that this would not be feasible for large states.

In modern times, more and more additional levels of advisory boards, expert committees and working groups are involved; in addition, the influence of associations and lobbies is increasing. Political issues are increasingly complex and difficult to understand. These additional expert levels have relevant influence on decisions, but are not elected by the people and have therefore no direct democratic legitimacy. Some authors even believe that the age of **post-democracy** has begun, where a state is formally conducted by democratic rules, but whose application is progressively limited in practice.

Scharpf is concerned that this development together with financial constraints undermines democracy because the margin for alternative decisions is decreasing and more and more predefined by experts. **Habermas** is missing normative visions in the political theories. A similar discussion was already ongoing when the political system of Western Germany consisted only of three parties and the resulting lack of alternatives was seen as danger.

NGOs and experts have the advantage to provide knowledge and expertise without pressure by elections and by also provide continuity that does not exist in parliaments, but such groups can mutate to 'parallel governments' (**Kielmannsegg, Eschenburg**).

Others argue that civil society and governance concepts will motivate more associations and lobbies to involve themselves even more, i.e. make things worse. But according to **Dahl**, power executed by multiple actors (**polyarchy**) helps to keep the democracy stable by a balance of power; otherwise a single actor may overcome all others. On the other hand, the number of relevant actors should not be too large to avoid confusion in political communication (refer to Czada).

3.4.4 Governance and Civil Society

Civil society can have different meanings. The EU has a conventional approach where the classic non-governmental political actors form the civil society (White book Governance), i.e. churches and religious communities, trade unions, employers' organizations and NGOs. Other authors focus more on the **third sector**, i.e. all parts of the society that are neither state nor market. Also, some authors summarize all NGOs as civil society.

In international affairs, civil society is also used as term for transition of former dictatorships where the state was doing everything and did not accept non-governmental structures or activities in the past.[5]

The current concepts of civil society have many roots:

- Social movements since the 1980ies
- Increasing activities of local and international NGOs
- Community Foundations, Corporate Citizenship, Corporate Social Responsibility as private initiatives to support the society
- **Communitarianism** was originally developed by **Amitai Etzioni** and emphasizes the need to balance individual rights and interests with that of the community as a whole. The individual is embedded in the community and solidarity and neighborly help are important elements.

These concepts may be demanding, because citizens are expected to feel responsible for others, be tolerant, open for dialogues, showing solidarity, willing to share etc. etc. Some authors believe that this is an increasing **overstretch of the middle class**: On one side, there is no more job security, net wages do not increase anymore and people have to be very flexible, but on the other hand they should be more motivated to help others. This debate is overlapping with the debate on **work-life-balance** and also with the **gender mainstreaming** debate where e.g. equal job chances for women (in particular mothers) are discussed.

However, there are cultural differences: historically, the Anglo-American culture supports the concept of self-responsibility and lean state[6] while in continental Europe there is a tradition that many people rely on and trust the state and expect help and guidance even if this requires some interventions and controls.

Some authors argue that the role of civil societies will be affected by contrary developments such as:

---

[5] There are ongoing dispute about the character of this transition:
- this is a modernization process that cannot be stopped by the old elites in the long run ('Western perspective')
- this is a Trojan horse to weaken Eastern States and get their energy resources and commodities under control ('Eastern perspective')
- the end of the process is unknown, this may or may not result in modern democracies and market economies (descriptive position, Huntington/Nohlen)

[6] But in UK there is debate that New Labour has implemented a „Nanny State" with an extensive control level.

- Erosion of values and traditions in many societies, individualization, hedonism, patchwork biographies, increasing divorce rate, broken families, single fathers and mothers
- Insecure jobs and increased mobility requirements may destroy the material basis for volunteerism and long-term commitments
- Increase of disadvantaged groups and integration problems in many countries
- Financial crisis of many churches and religious communities in particular in Europe led to a significant reduction of services and activities (such as closure of abbeys and churches)
- Some authors argue that community foundations only fill gaps that are caused by state failure, i.e. this is a sign of crisis
- Communitarianism may also be used as an instrument to control individual ways of life by the community.

3.4.5 Good Governance

The Organization for Economic Co-operation and Development (OECD) has formulated widely accepted criteria for **Good Governance**: Respect for the rule of law; openness, transparency and accountability to democratic institutions; fairness and equity in dealings with citizens, including mechanisms for consultation and participation; efficient, effective services; clear, transparent and applicable laws and regulations; consistency and coherence in policy formation; and high standards of ethical behavior.

Developing countries sometimes criticize that Good Governance requirements are primarily directed against them but not against undemocratic powerful states, i.e. who is poor and weak, is part of the debate while all others are not.

However, there are also concepts that industrialized Western countries should not act as military or as trade powers, but act in a civil manner, i.e. try to solve problems via communication and negotiations in a fair manner (**civil state** concept; Simonis).

4. International Relations - Some Recent Developments

4.1 From Globalization to Regionalization?

The globalization is not really new, international trade was already existing in ancient times and e.g. in the 15th century between Europe, Asia, Africa and Asia. After the conquest of Constantinople in 1453 by the Ottoman Empire, naval expeditions were financed to bypass the Ottomans, which resulted in missions like **Vasco da Gamas** tour around Africa and **Columbus'** discovery of America in 1492. In the 15th century, China also had a powerful fleet led by **Zheng He**, but the government stopped sea activities later on.

In the first phase, Spain and Portugal were the leading countries, and then England and The Netherlands emerged as new sea powers. Then, the focus was driven on direct control and ownership of territories which is known as **colonialism/imperialism.** The most territories were controlled by the United Kingdom and France.

Between World War I and II, the **League of Nations** existed, but as only a small part of the world consisted of fully independent nations, it was not really a global organization. Moreover, the USA did not join which was a major drawback.

As a consequence of World War II, a global political, legal and economic framework was established and this was the starting point of the actual globalization.

The most important institutions are the **United Nations Organization** UNO since 1945 and the so-called **Bretton Woods-Institutions** such as the International Monetary Fund IMF, the World Bank and the General Agreement on Trade on Tariffs GATT since 1948. The GATT negotiations reduced the average levels of customs/duties/fees on imported goods remarkably (about 40% when GATT started to about 8% around 2000) and stimulated global trade.

The growth of global relationships was supported by lowered transportation costs and low energy and commodity costs in the 1960ies and 1970ies. Improved planes and ships were a technical factor which positively interacted with the also increasing tourism.

In addition to the economic dimension, Globalization has three further dimensions:
- **Environment:** climate change, protection of species and tropical rain forest are some of many problems.
- **Social dimension:** social standards are under pressure by immigration and also by outsourcing of companies in cheaper low-level countries.
- **Culture:** there is also an increasing cultural exchange between all parts of the world (music, food etc.). However, if only the revenues of media production are taken, American culture is clearly dominating as shown by media studies of the European Union.

The first crisis of globalization started in 1971. Until this year, currencies were linked to a Gold-Dollar system which resulted in stable exchange rates for many years. However, the expenses of the Vietnam War made it necessary to cancel the Gold-Dollar-system. After the first oil crisis of 1973, the **G7** as group of 7 largest industry nations (US, UK, France, Germany, Italy, Canada and Japan) was founded to manage the confusion that resulted from oil price shock and also from the end of the Gold-Dollar system that led to unstable and floating exchange courses. In Europe, the **European Currency System** was initiated in the 1970ies which finally led to the common currency **Euro** in 1992.

The end of the cold war between West and East in 1990 led to the end of the Communist system in Eastern Europe as separate economy[7]. This, and the democratization and growth of international agreements and organizations, stimulated the expansion of global trade and multinational companies (Global Players). Also, the so-called **tiger states** (a term that was not clearly defined, many authors included South Korea and Taiwan there, some others also included Singapore and its neighbors Indonesia and Malaysia) experienced a significant growth of their economies. In 2001, the term **BRIC** was created for the four large countries Brazil, Russia, India and China that are now major competitors of the G7 states.

The 1990ies were an era of liberalization and enhanced globalization which resulted in the creation of the **World Trade Organization (WTO)** as successor of the GATT.

---

[7] Scientific contacts, exchange of knowledge and travel were restricted during cold war between West and East. Moreover, Eastern money was primarily used as accounting unit and was not convertible, i.e. could not be used for international payments.

This decade was optimistic, even the **'end of history'** was proclaimed, i.e. the end of massive confrontation between military powers.

The Internet as a technical platform accelerated the exchange between regions and also between financial markets. All factors together caused a massive expansion and interaction between financial markets, resulting in an increase of the New York Stock Exchange Index Dow Jones Industrial Average from 3.000 points in 1990 to 10.000 points in 1999. The expansion of the financial markets was also driven by the increasing credit volume for estates and the release of **derivates**, i.e. financial instruments that are derived from some other asset, index, event, value or condition (known as the underlying asset). Finally, this was an overexpansion (**bubble**) and led to the **Financial Crisis** in 2008/2009.

The era of regionalization

However, the rise of the BRIC, the increasing prices for oil and commodities and the terror act of 9/11 (World Trade Center attack on 11 Sep 2001) led to a revised perspective, now regionalization, security policy and industrial policy are the new matters.

There was further progress in globalization and **Dubai** emerged as a new financial market in the Gulf Region, but the Financial Crisis in 2008/2009 caused a severe crisis of globalization with increased debts, reduced trade and a decrease in migration.

The regional economic cooperations (such as the EU, NAFTA, Mercosur, ASEAN and Ecowas) follow more and more their own interests. The lack of resources and the increased industry espionage[8], the violation of patents and copyrights are some of the reasons for increasing tensions. Therefore, states try to support ‚national champions' in strategic key industrial sectors and try to keep foreign investors outside these areas (**industrial policy**). Market protection (**protectionism**) is also under discussion again.

Terrorism, prevention of international crime and money laundering and human trafficking are reasons for more controls in international travel.

---

[8] According to the **theory of knowledge-based societies** industrial countries with low resources need better knowledge and high quality products to be competitive. A loss of knowledge and qualified people is a major threat for those countries.

A special problem are **failed states** with a lack of functioning institutions which leads to insufficiently controlled areas which may cause danger for international trade as well[9].

More and more, immigration is seen as a danger for stability of societies; therefore the EU agency Frontex tries to stop immigration by preventive actions. The US has similar issues in particular with Mexico. However, the migration within the continents is increasing and some authors argue that immigrants are urgently needed human resources in particular in aging societies. They ask for **legalization** of illegal immigrants who are already working in a country to allow their social integration. Some countries did this already while others do not.

The regionalization is therefore an economic process which is accompanied by major changes in security policy. After a short overview on international organizations, the most important economic organizations and some recent developments in security policy are discussed.

4.2 International Organizations

4.2.1 Introduction
The number of international organizations has increased as a part of the globalization process. Increasing problems (military, economy/developmental aid and environment are the main three areas) and the increasing interactions between states are factors that support the foundation of new organizations.

There are three main groups of international organizations:
- Die UN and their specialized agencies (e.g. Food and Agriculture Organization of the United Nations (FAO) or the United Nations Educational,

---

[9] The most cited example is Somalia, where is no state in theory, but in real life there are 5 regions with the well-working Republic of Somaliland since 1991, three *autonomous regions Puntland, Maakhir and Galmudug* and the remaining former Somalia with the capital Muqdisho, where the official government is (or should be) located, however the **al-Shabaab** rebels are controlling most of this area. Lack of control allows illegal fishery of foreign boats, but also increasing piracy. However, things are complex, as there is a lot of oil in Somalia and this is the reasons why there is only limited cooperation in the international community (with several not fully coordinated military missions) and only limited attempts to eradicate piracy.

Scientific and Cultural Organization (UNESCO) and related organizations (e.g. International Atomic Energy Agency (IAEA)
- the Bretton Woods-organizations WTO, International Monetary Fund and World bank (Economic aspects) who are also related UNO organizations
- and globally acting NGOs like Amnesty International, Transparency International and Greenpeace.

A new type of globally acting NGOs are small, but well-capitalized and influential **foundations**, e.g.
- **Bill** and **Melinda Gates Foundation**: 33.4 billion dollars (2008). The owner of the investment company Berkshire Hathaway **Warren Buffett** plans to add further 30 billion dollars to this foundation.
- **Open Society Institute** of the stock trader and financial expert **George Soros** that supports the transition of former Soviet Union states; some of these states suspected the institute to be involved into reform movements in various states
- **Wellcome Trust** (linked to pharmaceutical company Glaxo-Wellcome): 26.1 billion dollars are available for medical research.

The most international organizations are small. The large majority of people in international organizations work for the UNO and their agencies/related organizations or for the European Union.

4.2.2 The United Nations Organization UNO

The Charter of the UNO established six principal organs: the General Assembly, the Security Council, the Economic and Social Council, the Trusteeship Council, the International Court of Justice, and the Secretariat. In addition, there are 15 specialist agencies, and several programs and related organizations which are linked to the UNO by agreements. The UNO has specialized agencies (e.g. Food and Agriculture Organization of the United Nations (FAO) or the United Nations Educational, Scientific and Cultural Organization (UNESCO) and related organizations, e.g. the International Atomic Energy Agency (IAEA).

The General Assembly of all 192 Member states accepts new members, is responsible for budget and elects the non-permanent members of the **Security Council** that is composed of five permanent members: China, France, Russia, the United Kingdom and the United States and the non-permanent members. The Assembly also elects the members of the Economic and Social Council (ECOSOC) and the judges of the International Court of Justice (ICJ) in Den Haag. The United Nations Secretariat is headed by the Secretary General (now by Ban Ki-moon).

4.2.3 The Bretton Woods-Institutions

As a consequence of the Greet Depression in the 1930ises and the World War II, the conference of allied nations in Bretton Woods established the International Monetary Fund (IMF) and the International Bank for Reconstruction and Development (IBRD), which today is part of the World Bank Group. These organizations became operational in 1945 after a sufficient number of countries had ratified the agreement.

The third "Bretton-Woods-Institution" was the **International trade organization (ITO)** but the US congress was hesitant to agree. Instead, the **GATT General Agreement on Tariffs and Trade** was implemented, which was only part IV of the Havana Charta of 1948 which was the planned basis of the ITO.

The Bretton Woods system obliged each country to maintain the exchange rate of its currency within a fixed value plus or minus one percent in terms of gold. In practice, this was a **Gold-Dollar system**, i.e. there were fixed exchange rates to the Dollar and in theory people could change Dollar into Gold. As a consequence of the Vietnam War expenses the US were not able to maintain the Gold-Dollar system and the system collapsed in 1971, after the United States unilaterally terminated convertibility of the dollar to gold.

At the end of the cold war 1990, it was possible to expand the GATT to the new organization World Trade Organization (WTO) in 1995 which also covered now new areas, the services (**GATS**) and intellectual property rights (**IPR**) such as patents (**TRIPS**). GATT, GATS and TRIPS are the three main agreements, but in total there are more than 60 agreements.

The IMF and World Bank system[10] is funded by various, mainly Western countries who tried to link credits to developing countries to a strict budgetary discipline which led to a lot of disputes in particular in the 1990ies.

---

[10] The world bank group consists of International Bank for Reconstruction and Development – IBRD; also: 'World Bank', the International Development Association – IDA, the International Finance Corporation – IFC, the Multilateral Investment Guarantee Agency – MIGA and the International Centre for Settlement of Investment Disputes – ICSID.

Tab. 5 The Bretton Woods System

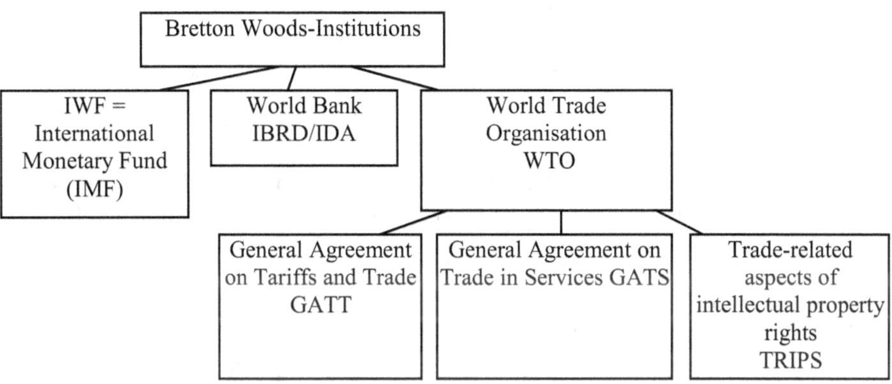

The GATS agreement covers four modes of supply for the delivery of services in cross-border trade:

Mode 1: Cross-border supply

Mode 2: Consumption abroad

Mode 3: Commercial presence

Mode 4: Presence of a natural person (service delivered within the territory of the Member, with supplier present as a natural person). There is criticism that mode 4 may lead to uncontrolled immigration and erosion of social standards if fully implemented. However, member states have still the right to protect service sectors such as the health care system.

The **Intellectual Property Rights (IPR)** policy deals with patents, copyright, design, brands and utility patents. The USA as leading nation with regard to new patents promoted the patent protection and was able to establish a 20-year protection period in the TRIPS agreement and Western countries fight against **product privacy** (illegal copies of protected goods). There is a dispute between US and China, as US argues that Chinese government should do more against product piracy while China argues that they enhanced their efforts already.

An important instrument of the GATT/WTO are bilateral most favored nation clauses (**MFN clauses**) which led to stepwise reduction of average customs/duty rates from 40% to 8% since 1945. If a country provides a MFN clause to one WTO member, it has to offer this to all other WTO members as well. Meanwhile, the WTO has 153 members, representing more than 95% of total world trade and 30 observers, most of them seeking membership.

In case of disputes, parties can ask for a consultation/mediation within the WTO and then ask for a panel process where a formal panel report is established. Either side can appeal a panel's ruling. The appeal can uphold, modify or reverse the panel's legal findings and conclusions. Normally appeals should not last more than 60 days, with an absolute maximum of 90 days. The **Dispute Settlement Body (DSB)** within the WTO has to accept or reject the appeals report within 30 days and rejection is only possible by consensus appeal.

At the beginning of the GATT, the USA was the leading nation and could therefore solve problems during negotiations. This shadow of hierarchy was necessary due to the **consensus principle**, i.e. agreements could only be made when all members agreed. Meanwhile, the process of regionalization has taken place and more and more regional groups try to achieve their own goals. This makes agreements meanwhile almost impossible. In the current trade negotiation called the Doha Development Agenda (or **Doha Round**) since 2001, there is permanent disagreement between rich and poor countries in particular with regard to conditions of agrarian trade.

Structure of WTO negotiations 2008 (acc. to Financial Times Germany)
There are overlapping alliances with conflicting and overlapping interests which makes communication and problem solving extremely difficult. Therefore, the **'greenroom'** was established as a smaller communication circle to clarify issues upfront.

Tab. 6 WTO negotiations

Expert Committees			
Agriculture	Industry	Trade rules and anti-dumping	Trade and IPR issues
WTO General Director Pascal Lamy as Coordinator			
'Greenroom' 30 ministers who should representative all relevant alliances within the WTO			
	EU27 G7 G10 industrial countries who want to protect the agrarian markets African, Caribbean and Pacific Group of States (ACP) ca. 50 states Group of Twenty (largest developing countries)		
Trade Negotiations Committee (TNC) as formal decision body of the 153 member st			

G20 as a new global actor

In 1999, a new group, the group of the 20 most important industrial and developing countries, the G20 emerged (not be mixed up with the 'Group of Twenty' of largest developing countries), which is an informal group of 19 states plus the European Union. The G20 covers 2/3 of the world population, 90% of the gross domestic product and 80% of the world trade. During financial crisis, this was the most relevant actor, as the chiefs of the national central banks, the finance ministers, the president of the European Central Bank and also other delegates e.g. from IMF took participated in the meetings.

But without a leading nation as shadow of hierarchy that could enforce agreements or end deputes, this did not work as expected. There were a lot of declarations, but the practical relevance was far beyond expectations. During crisis, US and China were the most relevant actors, China as largest holder of currency reserves and US as largest debtor. Therefore, the discussion whether the future may be dominated by a **G2** between China and USA has started.

54

4.3 Economic Communities

The most complex organization is the European Union (EU) which may end up in a European state in future, so this organization is presented in detail.

There are other powerful economic regional organizations that are presented below. As a relatively new organization, the **Shanghai Cooperation Organization SCO** was created. The SCO has both economic and security goals. Therefore, the SCO is also presented here.

4.3.1 The European Union

4.3.1.1 Structure and Legislation

The European Union officially consists of 27 member states with almost 500 million citizens, but as shown later, the EU influences even more states.

The EU began with **European Coal and Steel Community ECSC** formed among six countries in 1951 (France, Belgium, Italy, Germany, The Netherlands and Luxembourg) and the **Treaty of Rome** in 1957 by the same states which led to the **European Economic Community EEC** and **Euratom** for cooperation with regard to nuclear energy as shown below.

Tab. 7 European Union

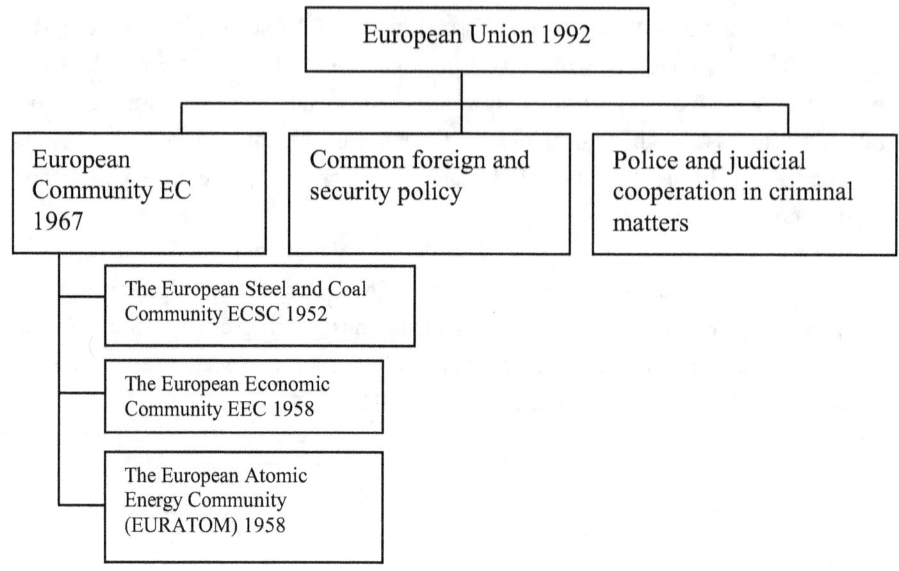

In 1967 the Merger Treaty created a single set of institutions known as the European Communities (**EC**), but often the simple term **European Community** is used instead. Please note that the European Coal and Steel Community ECSC was only a 50-year-treaty. In 2002, the ECSC was fully absorbed by the EC.

After the cold war, the **European Union** with three '**pillars**' was created by the **Treaty of Maastricht**, the EC was now the first pillar in the new organization. There were already some activities in the areas of security policy and police cooperation, but now this was fully established.

Several enlargements (inclusion of new member states) resulted in 27 instead of 6 member states. Only Greenland, an autonomous province of Denmark has left the EU in 1985 to protect the fish resources.

To join the EU, a country must meet the **Copenhagen criteria** from 1993; this is a stable democracy that respects human rights and the rule of law; a functioning market economy and the acceptance of the obligations of membership, including EU law.

Until the **Treaty of Lisbon** that came into operation in December 2009, the EU consisted of three 'pillars'. The first pillar was **supranational**, i.e. there was a political level above the nation states with the **European Commission**, the **European Parliament** and the **European Council** as a European administrative level above the nation states (like the Champions League above the national premier leagues' in soccer/football).

The second pillar (security and foreign policy) and the third pillar (police and justice) were **intergovernmental**, i.e. the member states made common decisions and actions.

In future, almost all issues will be managed with the system of the first pillar.

The main supranational institutions of the EU are:

The **European Commission** is the executive of the Union and is responsible for drafting all law of the European Union and legislative initiative.

From a formal point of view, Europe is not a state, but practically, the **European Commissioners** are like 'European ministers'. The president of the commission is bit like a 'European prime minister'. Each commissioner is supported by administrative units; most important are the **General Directions** which are like

'European ministries'. As in national states, ministries delegate technical and expert issues to lower administrative levels. In the European Union, these are the **agencies**.

While the commission is drafting and executing law, the decision whether a law comes into action is usually made together by the **European Parliament** and the **Council of Ministers** (of the member states) as a so-called '**co-decision**' (i.e. either both bodies agree or the legal act cannot be released). This process is also known as **Community method** or meanwhile also known as **ordinary legislation method**. In the past, the parliament had less influence, and the vote could often be overridden by the Council, but meanwhile the co-decision is clearly the dominant way to make decisions.

The **European Parliament** started historically with nominated delegates, but is meanwhile regularly elected and consists of the elected members of national parties. Most of these parties form **European party federations** which are dominating the European Parliament which has 785 members. The representation of countries is not fully proportional, i.e. very small countries are overrepresented to give them a real chance for political participation. The largest party federations are:
- European People's Party (Christian Democrats) and European Democrats 288 members
- Socialist Group 215 members
- Alliance of Liberals and Democrats for Europe 101 members
- Union for Europe of the Nations (conservative) 44 members
- Greens/European Free Alliance 43, but there are further smaller groups as well

The work of the parliament is supported by two committees bodies, the **Economic and Social Committee** and the **Committee of the Regions** which are however of limited practical relevance (as they consist of nominated delegates which have very different backgrounds so these committees are rather heterogeneous).

The Council of the European Union (informally known as the **Council of Ministers** or just the Council) presents the member states and is the main decision making body of the Union. However, top-level decisions and general directions are made by the **European Council** which is the group of heads of state or government of the EU member states.

When a law comes into force, the Commission is responsible for execution and is supported and supervised by committees controlled by the Council, this procedure is called **comitology**.

Before a law is suggested by the Commission, the Commissions often makes general suggestions called **White Books**.
Then, so-called **Green Books** give more details and the Councils may make **decisions** that ask the Commission to do something in a certain area. Council and Commission can enhance this by **action plans**. Nevertheless, only the Commission has the legislation initiative, otherwise nothing happens.

There are two levels of European Law. **Primary European law** is the group the treaties which define the competencies of the European Union. The **secondary law** is the sum of regulations released by the EU. This comprises **regulations** (legal acts which are effective directly for each citizen in the EU), **directives** (legal acts which must be taken over by national states, but their parliaments have to agree here), and **decisions** (e.g. anti-trust decisions). The sum of European law is also called 'Acquis'.

The judicial branch of the EU is called the **Court of Justice** of the European Union and is responsible for interpretation of European law and its application. In general, the court emphasizes the precedence of European law over national legislation and is often called the **motor of European integration**.
The most powerful person in the second and third pillar was the **Secretary-General of the Council of the European Union**, because this person is also the **High Representative for Common Foreign and Security Policy** (the second pillar). This representative is a kind of 'European foreign minister'.

Please note that in former times the legislative procedures were only valid for the first pillar, in the second and third pillar the actions were usually based on agreements between the national governments. Since December 2009, the pillar system is cancelled and now the procedures of the first pillar are now applicable for almost all areas in the EU.

The EU is still not a state, but due the **Treaty of Lisbon** the High Representative will get now an own corps of diplomats as part of a kind of 'European foreign office'.

4.3.1.2 General Trends in the EU

General trends in the EU are:

- Permanent expansion of responsibilities
- Go away from detailed directives to framework regulation, technical matters were handed over to expert level (EU agencies)
- Instead of a one-step harmonization of national legislation, a more stepwise convergence approach was chosen after the memorandum of Sir Ralf **Dahrendorf** in 1973
- Increase of voluntary initiatives that are not mandatory for each member anymore (such as the Euro, the Schengen agreement etc.). Despite official denial, there many examples for a multi-speed Europe or **two-speed Europe** (called also **variable geometry Europe** or **Core Europe** depending on the form it would take in practice)
- However, there is permanent progress to a European state (despite official denial). The **Treaty of Lisbon** is an important step forward.
- Influence on states outside the EU by Euro and on other states by the **European Economic Area EEA.**

These trends are described in more detail in the following sections.

4.3.1.3 Permanent Expansion of Responsibilities

The so-called '**competence of competence**' is still the matter of the national states, i.e. the EU cannot expand their responsibilities. However, if the competence is given to EU, it is away and cannot be retracted. This is called '**bolt effect**'. There is no Master plan of European unification, but the large number of initiatives and decisions creates an ,integration pressure'. During development of EU, nation states discover additional areas for possible activities (**Upgrading of common interests** acc. to **Haas**).

4.3.1.4 Change from Detailed Guidance to Framework Guidance

As a response to the increasingly complex matters within the EU, their governance strategy is focused on five goals: *Openness, participation, accountability, effectiveness and Coherence.* These should be achieved by

- **Framework directives:** technical details should be regulated not in framework directives, but in secondary documents
- **Co-Regulation**: combine European rules and national rules where possible
- **Open method of co-ordination:** was established by the Treaty of Maastricht 1992. When EU member states agree to cooperate in sectors which are usually not part of the EU responsibility, this should be allowed
- Foundation of **autonomous EU regulation agencies** to delegate technical issues to the expert levels.

4.3.1.5 The European Agencies

The EU's agencies were related to the three pillars as **Community agencies** (first pillar), **Common Foreign and Security Policy agencies** (second pillar) and **Police and judicial cooperation in criminal matters agencies** (third pillar) or act as **Executive agencies** for the management of one or more Community programs. These agencies are set up for a fixed period and are located Brussels or Luxembourg.

The primary idea was to hand over ,low politics' matters to the agencies, but meanwhile agencies are accepted as successful solution to handle many policy areas, so the number of agencies is permanently increasing.

Agencies are distributed all over Europe which helps to involve and motivate the member states as the agencies provide highly paid and challenging jobs. Technical problems are delegated from the political to the technical expert-dominated level to disburden the politicians. Agencies do not take away competence from politicians, because politicians can override any agency decision, if needed, i.e. to disburden politicians does not mean to take power away from them.

Tab. 8 Agencies of the European Union

EU structure	Agencies
First pillar	Community Fisheries Control Agency (CFCA)
	Community Plant Variety Office (CPVO)
	European Agency for Safety and Health at Work (EU-OSHA)
	European Agency for the Management of Operational Cooperation at the External Borders (FRONTEX)
	European Aviation Safety Agency (EASA)
	European Centre for Disease Prevention and Control (ECDC)
	European Centre for the Development of Vocational Training (Cedefop)
	European Chemicals Agency (ECHA)
	European Environment Agency (EEA)
	European Food Safety Authority (EFSA)
	European Foundation for the Improvement of Living and Working Conditions (EUROFOUND)
	European GNSS Supervisory Authority (GSA)
	European Institute for Gender Equality (under preparation)
	European Maritime Safety Agency (EMSA)
	European Medicines Agency (EMEA)
	European Monitoring Centre for Drugs and Drug Addiction (EMCDDA)
	European Network and Information Security Agency (ENISA)
	European Railway Agency (ERA)
	European Training Foundation (ETF)
	European Union Agency for Fundamental Rights (FRA)
	Office for Harmonisation in the Internal Market (Trade Marks and Designs) (OHIM)
	Translation Centre for the Bodies of the European Union (CdT)
Second pillar	European Defence Agency (EDA)

Second pillar	European Union Institute for Security Studies (ISS)
	European Union Satellite Centre (EUSC)
Third pillar	European Police College (CEPOL)
	European Police Office (EUROPOL)
	The European Union's Judicial Cooperation Unit (EUROJUST)
Executive agencies	Education, Audiovisual and Culture Executive Agency (EACEA)
	European Research Council Executive Agency (ERC)
	Executive Agency for Competitiveness and Innovation (EACI)
	Executive Agency for Health and Consumers (EAHC)
	Research Executive Agency (REA)
	Trans-European Transport Network Executive Agency (TEN-T EA)

4.3.1.6 Convergence Instead of Harmonization

Instead of a one-step harmonization of national legislation, a more stepwise convergence approach was chosen after the **Dahrendorf memorandum** in 1973 which is also reflected by the slogan ‚**unity in diversity**' of the EU.

And if for technical reasons a harmonization has to be done, e.g. for the European driving license, long transition periods allow to use the old already existing licenses which makes it easier to change the documents (in the long run, only European driving licenses will exist anymore, because all new drivers get only the new documents).

4.3.1.7 A Europe of Two Speeds?

Despite official denial, there many examples for a multi-speed Europe or two-speed Europe, because there is a permanent increase of voluntary initiatives which are not mandatory for each member anymore.

- First pillar (economy): **Euro and European Central Bank ECB**. The euro (€) is the official currency of the European Union, and is currently in use in 16 of the 27 Member States. The states, known as the **Euro zone**, are since 2009 Austria, Belgium, Cyprus, Finland, France, Germany, Greece, Ireland, Italy, Luxembourg, Malta, the Netherlands, Portugal, Slovakia, Slovenia and Spain.

Outside the EU, the euro is also the sole currency of two former Yugoslavian states (Montenegro and Kosovo) and several European micro states (Andorra, Monaco, San Marino and Vatican City). In particular, many African states use the CFA Franc that is linked to France and therefore also linked to the Euro, i.e. large parts of Africa are also involved. Some French Pacific Territories use the **Colonies françaises du Pacifique (CFP)-Franc** that is also linked to the Euro.

- Second pillar (security): **European military missions,** e.g. EUCHAD in Chad 2008. There is a dispute whether these missions are an alternative to NATO or the establishments of a 'European pillar' within the NATO, most authors prefer the second opinion. Also increasing cooperation between secret agencies is reported in literature. These activities are historically based on the so-called **Western European Union WEU** which was the European pillar in the Western alliances during the cold war.

- Third pillar (Police and justice in criminal matters): The **Schengen Agreement** is a treaty signed in 1985 which allows reduced border controls between member states. Despite the concerns with regard to crime and illegal immigration, Schengen was successful and meanwhile various Non-EU states such as Switzerland and now Serbia joined. The **Treaty of Prüm** allows exchange of further data between signatory states, such as genetic fingerprints.

4.3.1.8 Are there 'informal' EU-Members?

Via the so-called **European Economic Area**, Iceland, Norway and Liechtenstein were closely linked to the EU and took over the large majority of EU laws (80%), Norway close to 100%. Switzerland has only limited relationships to the EU with 7 treaties, but is e.g. member of the Schengen agreement. These countries are also members of the **European Free Trade Area EFTA** which was originally founded as an alternative organization to the EU (all EFTA members claimed neutrality during cold war). Iceland did not want to join the EU directly due to fishery issues while Norway is afraid that the EU may get too much influence on their energy policy and reserves (this explains takeover of EU laws without joining the EU). After financial crisis, Iceland was almost bankrupt and has asked to join EU now.

European micro states (Andorra, Monaco, San Marino and Vatican City) are more or less completely integrated. Andorra was a condominium of France and Spain for 7 centuries; on 16 March 1993 Andorra became independent and is now partially involved in EU matters.

Since the 1960ies, Turkey tries to join the EU without success. The reasons are disputed: Some analysts argue that Turkey needs to improve the democratic institutions before joining, a second group believes that the true reason would be that Turkey is an Islamic state while the EU is Christian while a third group believes that the hidden agenda is that Turkey is simply 'too big to join'. Turkey would automatically have more parliament seats than most other state, would receive a lot of money from EU funds and would be a big player from the beginning.

4.3.1.9 The Treaty of Lisbon

The Treaty of Lisbon entered into force on 01 December 2009. It amends the Treaty on European Union (TEU, Maastricht; 1992) and the Treaty establishing the European Community (TEC, Rome; 1957). In this process, the TEC was renamed to **Treaty on the Functioning of the European Union** (TFEU).

Important changes are:

- The legislative power of the European Parliament increases, as the co-decision procedure with the Council of Ministers is now dominating. This procedure is now called ordinary legislative procedure. This was done, because there was much criticism with regard to **lack of democracy** and participation in EU procedures. However, the EU is often perceived as complex and even as boring and the participation in European elections is much lower than in national elections in many member states
- expansion of **Qualified Majority Voting** (QMV) in the Council of Ministers to replace unanimity as the standard voting procedure in almost every policy area
- the position of a long-term **President of the European Council** to present a united position on EU policies was created
- the pillar system was cancelled. However, the former second pillar (foreign and security policy) will continue to exist in another form. In an effort to ensure greater coordination and consistency in EU foreign policy, the Treaty of Lisbon will create a **High Representative of the Union for Foreign Affairs and Security Policy**. The new High Representative will also become a Vice-President of the Commission, the administrator of the **European Defense Agency** and will be in charge of a common Foreign Office or Diplomatic Corps for the Union

- In the Lisbon Treaty the distribution of competences in various policy areas between Member States and the Union is explicitly stated in the following three categories:
  Exclusive competence (only the EU makes directives and conclude international agreements)
  Shared competence (member States cannot exercise competence in areas where the EU has done so)
  Supporting competence (the EU can support, coordinate or supplement Member States' actions)
- European Union becomes a consolidated body with a legal personality and the EU replaces and succeeds the European Community.

The fifty-five articles of the **Charter of Fundamental Rights** (ChFR) list political, social, and economic rights for EU citizens. Under the Treaty of Lisbon, the Charter is legally binding (except for those member states with an opt-out for this provision). It is intended to make sure that European Union regulations and directives do not contradict the **European Convention on Human Rights** which is ratified by all EU Member States.

4.3.1.10 European Governance Outside the EU: The Bologna Process
It is important to know that by far not all activities in Europe are initiated or managed by the European Union. Another organization is the **Council of Europe** with 47 member States, i.e. almost all countries of the European continent. This organization is not to be confused with the EU institutions and is for example relevant for European television and broadcasting (there visible as '**Eurovision**').

Moreover, there are further multilateral activities agreed outside the EU. The purpose of the **Bologna process** is to create the European higher education area by making academic degree standards and quality assurance standards more comparable and compatible throughout Europe. The agreement was signed at the University of Bologna in Italy 1999 as Bologna declaration by Ministers of Education from 29 European countries. Meanwhile, 46 states, including Russia and Vatican, have joined and further governmental meetings have been held in Prague (2001), Berlin (2003), Bergen (2005), London (2007) and Leuven (2009).
The main concepts are:

- the three study phases Bachelor-Master-PhD (doctorate), also called 3+2+3-system are now established as a new standard, i.e. three phases should be sufficient until the doctorate, thereof 3+2 years (alternatively 4+1 years) for Bachelor and Master studies plus 3 further years for the doctorate which may awarded with a Philosophical Doctor degree, abbreviated as PhD
- ECTS-system (European Credit Transfer System, that regulates credit points for achievements during study)
- Graduate Schools (for doctorate phase)

It is a common misunderstanding that the Bologna Process is an EU initiative. The EU had released a directive for mutual recognition of university degrees in 1989 which was not easy to handle and therefore not successful in practice.

Please note that also large parts of research policy and institutions are *not* under control of the EU, these are large research institutions such as the Conseil Européen pour la Recherche Nucléaire (**CERN**; European Laboratory for Particle Physics) for nuclear physics and European Molecular Biology Organization (**EMBO**) for molecular biology. Also, the **European Patent Office EPO** is not based on the European Union, but on an international agreement.

4.3.2 NAFTA

The **NAFTA North American Free Trade Agreement** is a economic and free-trade agreement between US, Canada and Mexico. This was replacing the US-Canadian free-trade agreement in 1989 and is an intergovernmental agreement. When adding up the Gross Domestic Product GDP of its members, it is the largest trade block in the world.

The North American Free Trade Agreement (NAFTA) has two supplements, the North American Agreement on Environmental Cooperation (NAAEC) and the North American Agreement on Labor Cooperation (NAALC).

4.3.3 Mercosur

The **Mercosur (Mercado Común del Cono Sur, also Mercosul)** was established in 1991 by Argentina, Brazil, Paraguay and Uruguay by the Asunción-Agreement, associated states are: Chile (1996), Bolivia (1997), Peru (2003), Colombia (2004), Ecuador (2004), Venezuela's integration is under discussion. Its purpose is to promote free trade and the free movement of goods, people, and currency. The Council of the common market (Consejo Mercado Común) is the highest-level agency of Mercosur with authority to conduct its policy. The Common Market Group is the executive body of Mercosul, and is coordinated by the Ministries of Foreign Affairs of the member states and has several Work Subgroups. The Mercosur suffers from conflicts between the largest members Brazil and Argentina, but there are already agreements between Mercosur and EU

.

4.3.4 Cooperation Council for the Arab States of the Gulf (CCASG)

The Cooperation Council for the Arab States of the Gulf (CCASG), also known as the **Gulf Cooperation Council (GCC)** is a political and economic union involving the six Arab states Bahrain, Kuwait, Oman, Qatar, Saudi Arabia and the United Arab Emirates that was founded in 1981 as reaction on the Iranian revolution of the Persian Gulf and first steps to liberalization of trade were started already in 1982.

For 2010, a common currency was planned with the name **Chalidschi** but there are implementation problems since Saudi-Arabia wanted the central bank on its territory. Please note that the United Arab Emirates (UAE) consists of seven states, which are Abu Dhabi, Dubai, Sharjah, Ajman, Umm al-Quwain, Ras al-Khaimah and Fujairah. **Abu Dhabi** is by far the largest UAE emirate, while **Dubai** underwent a massive expansion during the last few years.

4.3.5 ASEAN

The **ASEAN** (Association of Southeast Asian Nations) was founded in 1967 by Thailand, Indonesia, Malaysia, the Philippines and Singapore then Brunei (1984) joined, and then Vietnam, Cambodia, Laos and Burma (Myanmar). In the 1990ies the cooperation was intensified and a secretariat is now managing 19 ministerial groups which are supported by committees and working groups. The intergovernmental character and the principle of non-intervention in the internal affairs of other states (Asian Way) are important. The ASEAN reported 2007, that free-trade agreements should come into force until 2013 with China, Japan, South Korea, India, Australia and New Zealand and until 2015 the ASEAN Community (Cebu declaration).

The free trade agreement with China comes into operation already at 01 Jan 2010 and the ASEAN free trade should be fully implemented in 2015.

4.3.6 ECOWAS

The Economic Community of West African States (ECOWAS) was founded by the Treaty of Lagos in 1975. Member states are Benin, Burkina Faso, Gambia, Ghana, Guinea, Guinea-Bissau, Ivory Coast, Cape Verde, Liberia, Mali, Niger, Nigeria, Senegal, Sierra Leone and Togo, main official languages are English and French.

The Treaty of Cotonou 1993 was a step towards to political integration with a common Court of Justice and a common West African parliament in 2001. In addition, there was a military intervention of the common force ECOMOG in Liberia during the civil war in the 1990ies.

Nigeria has more than 50% of the population and economic power of the community. Within the community, there is still a francophone organization with a common currency that is called **CFA-Franc** (Franc de la Communauté Financière d'Afrique). It has a fixed exchange rate to the Euro: 100 CFA francs = 1 French (nouveau) franc = 0.152449 euro; or 1 euro = 655.957 CFA francs. The CFA-Franc zone is divided into two subgroups that are both guaranteed by the French treasury (Trésor public).

The **CFA-Franc BCEAO** is the currency of Benin, Burkina Faso, the Ivory Coast, Guinea-Bissau, Mali, Niger, Senegal and Togo while the **CFA-Franc BEAC** of the Economic and Monetary Community of Central Africa is used for Cameroon, Central African Republic, Chad, Republic of the Congo, Equatorial Guinea and Gabon.

The role of the CFA Franc is disputed: while some authors believe that this is mainly an instrument to keep the member states under French control, other authors emphasize the long-term stability and reliability of this system.

The European Central Bank is *not* responsible for those regions, however the Euro is strictly fixed to the CFA-Franc and therefore there is a factual linkage between the EU and Africa. It was discussed to introduce a common currency called **Eco** in the ECOWAS, which is now postponed to 2015.

Another important African economic organization is **The Southern African Customs Union (SACU),** a customs union that was already founded in 1910 with the Republic of South Africa, Botswana, Lesotho, Swaziland and Namibia as members. There are more organizations such as the Community of Sahel-Saharan States (CEN-SAD) and the Common Market for Eastern and Southern Africa

(COMESA) with partially overlapping memberships, in summary there is an increasing cooperation in Africa.

4.3.7 Shanghai Cooperation Organization SCO

The Shanghai Cooperation Organization (SCO) is an intergovernmental mutual-security organization which was founded in 2001 in Shanghai by China, Kazakhstan, Kyrgyzstan, Russia, Tajikistan, and Uzbekistan. Except for Uzbekistan, the other countries had been members of the **Shanghai Five**, founded in 1996.

In June 2002, the heads of the SCO member states met in Saint Petersburg, Russia to sign the SCO Charter.

The **Council of Heads of State** is the top decision-making body in the SCO. This council meets at the SCO summits, which are held each year in one of the member states' capital cities. The Foreign Ministers also meet regularly.

In 2004 the SCO decided to implement the Regional Anti-Terrorist Structure (RATS), headquartered in Tashkent, Uzbekistan, as a permanent organ of the SCO which serves to promote cooperation of member states against the **three evils of terrorism, separatism and extremism**. The Head of RATS is elected to a three-year term.

Outside the SCO framework, a joint military exercise between China and Russia, called Peace Mission 2005 was conducted and there were discussions that the SCO may take over a military role in the future. The joint military exercise in 2007 took place in Chelyabinsk; a further joint exercise took place in 2009.

The main goals are:
- to build trust between member states
- to enhance cooperation on technological, economic, ecologic, cultural areas and also in tourism, in particular to cooperate in the sectors of trade, energy and transport
- to keep peace and security of the region.

Some Western authors believe that there are hidden goals (but SCO denies):
- to roll back Western influence
- to fight against influence of Islam
- to control regional energy and economy and

- to eliminate NGOs from their territories.

However, SCO is still developing its structures so things may change in the future. It is discussed to invite India to become a full member. India, Pakistan and Iran already have an observer status.

4.3.8 The Rise of the BRIC

In economics, BRIC is an acronym that refers to the fast-growing developing economies of the large countries Brazil, Russia, India, and China. The acronym was first used by Goldman Sachs in 2001. The four countries, combined, may get stronger than the G7 in 2050, maybe even much earlier.

The BRICs are not organized as an economic bloc, or a formal trading association, but in 2009, the leaders of the BRIC countries held their first summit in Yekaterinburg, and issued a declaration calling for the establishment of a multipolar world order. Some authors believe that Mexico and South Korea should be mentioned also, some others believe that Indonesia maybe a dynamic newcomer.

Some reasons for the rise of these countries are presented below:

- Brazil: a large provider of soft and hard (iron) commodities and also with assumed large oil reserves.
- Russia: large oil and gas reserves, in particular in the north while industry still requires further modernization
- India: service provider and think tank for IT industry (e.g. software and data management in Bangalore) and e.g. the largest pharmaceutical generics provider of the World
- China: often called the "work bench" of the world with low wages that attract many companies to produce there (but increasing pressure e.g. by Vietnam based on their **DoiMoi** initiative) and many potential consumers in the own country. China is the largest currency reserve holder of the world.

For a long-lasting economic growth, the following factors seem to be essential:

- Macroeconomic stability (i.e. control of inflation etc.)
- Strong and stable political institutions
- Openness for trade and foreign investments
- High educational standards
- Demographic window: this is the period where the growth of population supports the growth of economy. This is the case, when less than 30% are under

15 years and less than 15% over 65 years. Brazil and China have passed this stage already while in India 30% are under 15 years.

4.4 Cooperation or Confrontation?

4.4.1 Industrial Policy

Industrial policy is a part of the economic policy. The principal objective of industrial policy is to establish the conditions that maintain the industrial sector's competitiveness and increase its potential for growth, employment and innovation. In the Treaty of Maastricht of 1992 the EU stated that the EU needs to keep their industry competitive. However, in the era of liberalization and globalization in the 1990ies, many authors interpreted industrial policy as an old-fashioned and protectionist approach. In 2004, the EU member states Germany, France and UK asked for a more proactive European industry policy.

The German ministry of economy mentioned three reasons in 2008:

- International **Hedge Funds** and **Private Equity enterprises** have collected much investment capital which can be used for global investments.
- There are new powerful competitors like China and India which cannot be ignored.
- The owners of energy resources have used the profits to build states funds that buy shares of large companies. In the long run, they may have a significant influence on national economies.

Tab. 9 State Funds

Country	Fund	billion US-Dollars 2008	Found ed in	basis
United Arab. Emirates	Abu Dhabi Investment Authority (ADIA)	875	1976	Oil
Singapore	Government of Singapore Investment Corporation (GIC)	330	1981	others
Norway	Government Pension Fund - Global (GPFG)	322	1990	Oil

Saudi-Arabia	Various funds	300	NA	Oil
Kuwait	Kuwait Investment Authority (KIA)	250	1953	Oil
China	China Investment Company Ltd.	200	2007	others
Russia	Stabilization Fund of the Russian Federation (SFRF)	144	2003	Oil

The European Union suggests establishing large market leading companies (e.g. by mergers) called **European Champions** to avoid too much influence of Non-EU countries. Some even argue that anti-trust rules in Europe are too strict to build up really large European companies. There is a lot of criticism that this policy undermines competition in the long run.

Key industries

As an example, the revision of the foreign trade and payments law of Germany (Außenwirtschaftsgesetz AWG) allows the government to evaluate and to forbid takeovers of strategic companies by foreign. However, the ministry has to consult the government before a denial comes into force. The critical limit for takeovers is 25% of a relevant company, but 'relevant' is not exactly defined to keep all options open.

4.4.2 Energy Policy

Energy policy is the policy of energy production, processing, distribution and consumption and has close links to economic, environmental, technology and security policy.

In particular, the European Union is dependent on energy imports from other countries, so energy policy is a major issue. Other countries like China also need to ensure future energy supply for the growing economy. As a result, there is an increasing competition between states.

In the EU, the national states are primarily responsible for energy policy, but the EU can influence this sector by many instruments, e.g. the common market (energy as priced good), environmental policy (carbon dioxide reduction), storage of energy reserves. Nevertheless, the position of the EU is weak due to the limited competencies. Nevertheless, the EU introduced the concept of **energy solidarity**, i.e. the member states should help each other.

In 2001, the European Union published the Green Book *Towards a European strategy for the security of energy supply*. Here, scenarios for a fictional 'EU-30' (EU 27 plus Turkey plus two former Yugoslavian republics) were presented. The curves were based on equivalents of million tons of crude oil units. A simplified version is given below:

Tab. 10 Energy balance

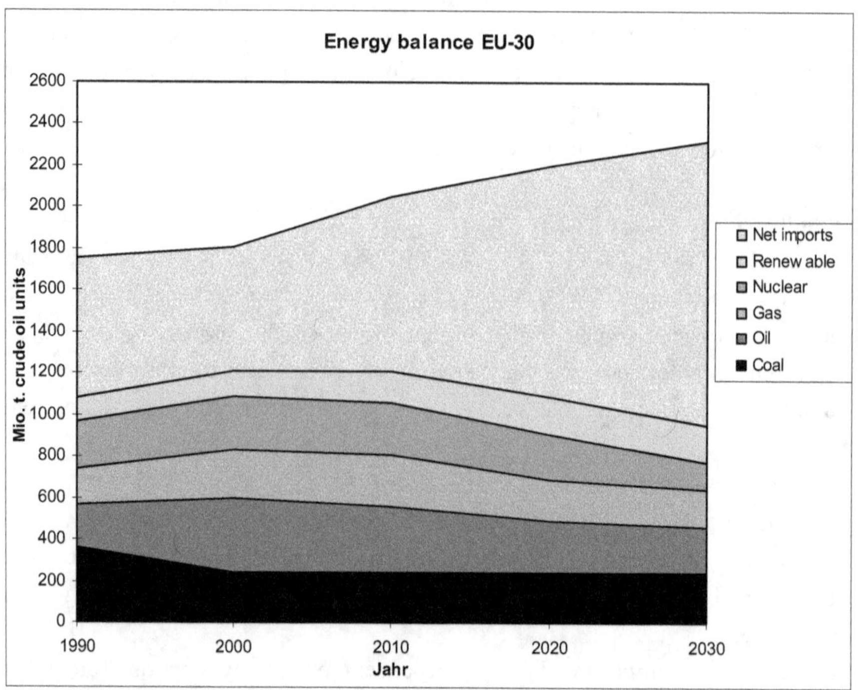

The results of the study were disappointing for the EU:

The dark zones show the declining European energy production while the striped lighter zone shows the increasing need for energy imports. Moreover, renewable energies may cover only a small portion of the needed energy and therefore nuclear energy may still be needed. A European study from 2004 showed the supposed producing countries that can cover Europe's energy needs.

Tab. 11 Main Energy Suppliers of the EU-27 in the year 2004

	Oil (%)	Gas (%)
[EU own production]	18	37
Russia	26	29
Norway	13	17
Saudi-Arabia	9	--
Libya	8	--
Iran	5	--

(source: EU-Commission)

However, meanwhile the focus is on **Nigeria** which may provide relevant amounts of oil and Liquid Natural Gas (LNG), but China also tries to buy these resources. Therefore, the main goals of the European Energy policy are:

• competitiveness
• sustainability
• security of supply

However, it is not possible to achieve all three goals with a single measure as shown in the table below:

Tab. 12 EU legislation for energy policy

Goal	Measures	Regulation/Policy
Reduction of energy consumption by 20% until 2020 by	technical norms	Directive on the Energy Performance of Buildings (2002/91/EC) Directive on energy end-use efficiency and energy services (2006/32/EC)
A more efficient utilization of energy	Increase energy costs by certificates and taxes	Directive 2003/96/EC restructuring the Community framework for the taxation of energy products and electricity Directive 2003/87/EC of the European Parliament and of the Council establishing a scheme for greenhouse gas emission allowance trading within the Community
	Research funding	Research: The Seventh Framework Program (2007-2013) Program Intelligent energy for Europe II with the subsets SAVE (buildings), ALTENER (renewable energy in production) and STEER (renewable energy in traffic) 780 Mio. Euro 2007-2013, EU-Agency: IEEA
Increase us of renewable energies until 2020 up to 20% to substitute conventional energy sources	Green electricity (e.g. solar technology) and – geothermal energy supported by subsidies or price guarantees	EU Renewable Electricity Directive (RES-E Directive) Directive on the promotion of cogeneration based on a useful heat demand in the internal energy market
Substitution	Financial support for biofuels	Directive on the promotion of the use of biofuels or other renewable fuels for transport EU Biomass Action Plan of December 2005

Diversification of energy sources	EU suggests to maintain atomic power plan	Mentioned e.g. in MEMO/07/7 Brussels, 10 January 2007 An energy policy for Europe: Commission steps up to the energy challenges of the 21st Century
Common European energy market	Transeuropean networks (TEN)	Project TEN. Some engineers are concerned that a common net could also produce EU-wide power failure in case of technical issues
	Separation of electricity nets and production	Still under discussion, the aim is to promote competition
Stockpiling	Council Directive 98/93/EC of 14 December 1998 amending Directive 68/414/EEC imposing an obligation on Member States to maintain minimum stocks: 90 days resources of the 3 most relevant oil sorts	
Relationships to producers	„energy dialogues" of the EU with producing countries (e.g. Russia, Algeria, Norway, Africa, Gulf states, OPEC) EU-partnership agreements with these countries	Partnership with Russia, Memorandum of Understandings with Algeria, Azerbaijan, Kazakhstan), regular consultations with Norway, Algeria will be associated to EU and free trade from 2017, EU consultation with Gulf states of the GCC, EU-Africa dialogues, Euro-Mediterranean Partnership (Barcelona-Process, EUROMED), European Neighbourship policy (ENP), 2005 energy cooperation with South Eastern Europe
	Try to bypass Russia via the Nabucco-Pipeline	
	Special national relationships in parallel to EU activities (e.g. France-Algeria, Germany-Norway), now contracts with Nigeria under discussion	

There are lots of strategic issues with regard to energy policy.

- Taxes and technical norms may make energy consumption more efficient and increase pressure on energy saving in the long run, in the short run this increases costs and makes economy less competitive
- Will research be successful in 50 years (nuclear fusion) or bring a sudden breakthrough tomorrow?
- Renewable energies are sustainable and make countries more independent from imports, but the climate does not allow the same amount of such energies in regions (wood/water: Sweden, sun: Spain)
- Price guarantees reduce the pressure to make a new technique more effective
- It would be much more effective to import sugarcane from Brazil for biofuel production than using European crop. But then the tropical rainforest may be reduced and the energy dependency of the EU would increase. On the other hand, it is deemed unethical to use crop for fuel, because this may lead to a shortage of cheap food as during the **Tortilla crisis** in Mexico
- Nuclear power has technological risks in particular in old nuclear plants and the atomic waste issue is still unresolved in the long run
- It seems attractive to have an anti-trust policy in the energy market, but fallen prices may enhance energy consumption
- EU Strategies for negotiations with producers are somewhat inconsistent: EU wants to have a partnership with Russia, but tries to bypass Russia at the same time by new pipelines....

<u>Conclusions (I)</u>

The three goals competitiveness, sustainability and security of supply cannot be achieved by a single measure; however you can try to achieve these goals stepwise. There are tensions between these three goals, but as you never know what the future brings try to achieve them all.

The producing countries have other problems, in particular:

- State-owned or private companies?: A state-owned company has the advantage that politicians can control everything, but it may have to pay the price for the learning curve if they don't have the expertise. A private company may offer a full service, but will look for its own profit

- High or low prices: high prices may motivate the consumers to look for alternatives, too low prices will lead to overexploitation
- Cartels or act on your own?: cartels may be more powerful, but may interfere with national policy
- Who should get what? Preferred provider contracts may lead to bilateral dependencies, because if the consuming country is in crisis and cannot pay anymore, this may have serious consequences for the provider, too.

Conclusions (II)

Also producing countries have strategic dilemmas which explain e.g. the permanent ups and downs in the OPEC. Also, an effective 'Gas-OPEC' could not be installed yet.

4.4.3 Resourcing Policy

There are three main groups of hard commodities that are now seen as limited resources by the politicians:

Tab. 13 Overview on Resources

Metals	Aluminum, Lead, Chromium, Iron, Cadmium, Cobalt, Copper, Lithium, Magnesium, Manganese, Molybdenum, Nickel, niobium (columbium), Tantalum, Titanium, Tungsten, Zinc, Tin
Precious metals	Gold, Palladium, Platinum, Rhodium, Silver
Industry minerals	Barite, Bentonite, Feldspar, Fluorspar, Gypsum and Anhydrite, Mica, Graphite, Potash, Kaolin, Phosphate, Silica, Sulfur, common salt, Cement, Zirconium

The most resources are not equally distributed all over the world and the 'Top 5' producing countries provide usually more than 50%, often more than 90% of the known production. Sometimes this is extreme: The German Government reported in 2007 e.g. that 45% of current lithium production is in Chile, 71.9% of Magnesium in China, 88.0% of Niobium (Colombium) in Brazil, 87.1% of Tungsten in China and 77.8% of Platinum in South Africa. As to be expected, countries with large territories have more resources. The following table shows the resources where large countries are the Top 5 providers.

Tab. 14 Large states as Top 5 providers

Country	Metal/Precious metal
Australia	Aluminum, Lead, Iron, Manganese, Nickel, Niobium, Tantalum, Titanium, Zinc, Silver
China	Aluminum, Lead, Iron, Cadmium, Lithium, Magnesium, Manganese, Molybdenum, Tungsten, Zinc, Tin, Gold, Silver
Brazil	Aluminum, Cobalt, Manganese, Niobium (Columbium), Tantalum, Tin
USA	Lead, Cupper, Lithium, Magnesium, Molybdenum, Zinc, Gold, Palladium, Platinum
Russia	Iron, Cobalt, Magnesium, Nickel, Tungsten, Palladium, Platinum, Rhodium

Rare metals such as colombium tantalite ('**Coltan**') are urgently needed for production of telecommunication and IT devices. This explains why states are increasingly nervous. Coltan mining is one of the issues in the civil war in Eastern regions of Congo.

The situation is similar for private companies. The top 5 companies control often more than 50% of the exploitation of a certain resource. End of 2008 there were e.g. *BHP Billiton (Australia), CVRD (Brazil), Alcoa, RioTinto (UK), Xstrata (China), AngloAmerican (UK) and Norilsk Nickel (Russia)*. In 2009, China tried to buy large companies and also resources in Australia which led to serious tensions between both countries.

4.4.3.1 The International Seabed Authority ISA

At the moment, the conquest and annexion of new territories is not enforceable and to get more control about resources **off-shoring** and **expansion to the poles** the only main options for expansion.

The **International Seabed Authority (ISA)** is an intergovernmental body based in Kingston, Jamaica, that was established to organize and control all mineral-related activities in the international seabed area beyond the limits of national jurisdiction, an area underlying most of the world's oceans. It is an independent treaty organization originally established by the **Law of the Sea Convention** a widely accepted multilateral treaty.

The exploration system came into operation in 2001 by 15-year contracts with organizations that had applied for specific seabed areas in the Pacific ocean to explore them for **polymetallic nodules.**

The eight current contractors are: Yuzhmorgeologya (Russian Federation); Interoceanmetal Joint Organization (IOM) (Bulgaria, Cuba, Slovakia, Czech Republic, Poland and Russian Federation); the Government of the Republic of Korea; China Ocean Minerals Research and Development Association (COMRA) (China); Deep Ocean Resources Development Company (DORD) (Japan); Institut français de recherche pour l'exploitation de la mer (IFREMER) (France); the Government of India, and the Federal Institute for Geosciences and Natural Resources of Germany.

The nodules are of high quality which makes their collection profitable despite the fact that they are lying on the ocean bed. Each contractor holds 2 areas; one area can be exploited, the other is reserved for research to avoid rapid overexploitation.

4.4.3.2 Race to the North Pole

1994 the ISA and the **United Nations Convention on the Law of the Sea** came into force. The convention defines how coastal nations can draw their territorial borders. Beyond the 12 nautical mile limit is the **contiguous zone**, in which a state could continue to enforce laws in four specific areas: pollution, taxation, customs, and immigration. **Exclusive economic zones (EEZs)** are zones from the edge of the territorial sea out to 200 nautical miles from the baseline. Within this area, the coastal nation has sole exploitation rights over all natural resources.

The continental shelf is defined as the natural prolongation of the land territory to the continental margin's outer edge, or 200 nautical miles from the coastal state's baseline, whichever is greater, but it cannot exceed 100 nautical miles beyond the 2,500 meter isobath (the line connecting the depth of 2,500 meters). The **Lomonosov Ridge** is an underwater ridge of continental crust in the Arctic Ocean and Russia claims this to be an extension of Russian territory. The claim and the supportive geologic evidence are disputed, because if this would be accepted, a large proportion of the Arctic Sea would be part of the Russian territory.

4.4.3.3 Antarctica

Various countries claim areas of Antarctica which covers 14 million km^2 (5.4 million square miles). Some countries have mutually recognized each other's territorial claims, but claims on Antarctica have been suspended since 1959 and the continent is considered politically neutral. Its status is regulated by the **Antarctic Treaty System**. Antarctica is now a scientific preserve and any military activity was banned. Currently, several countries have research stations there.

5. Security Policy

This section will introduce shortly the most important terms and issues.

There are many definitions in literature, a simple one is: *security is protection (prevention and defense) against any kind of threats.*

According to a widely used understanding of security, a state is secure, if the responsible authorities have enough rights, money and personnel to fight against threats. However, some authors support the concept that a society needs to be stable, otherwise it cannot be secure. This is a problem e.g. in military dictatorships, where the armed forces may even be the main danger for the current government.

The three main questions are:
- What are the current threats?
- What are the recent developments?
- What can be done?

The most frequently discussed threats are **Weapons of Mass Destruction (WMD), terrorism, organized crime/piracy, failed states** and **asymmetric wars, scarce energy** and **other resources, climate change**, issues of **demography** and **migration** and **digital technology**.

Weapons of Mass Destruction (WMD) are nuclear, biologic and chemical weapons. The main political problems are caused by countries that want to build nuclear weapons (**proliferation states**) and people who are willing to give this information (**proliferation networks**). For example, North Korea was able to develop nuclear bombs despite the political efforts of the USA to stop this. Many states are also concerned with regard to the advanced nuclear program of Iran as this threatens Israel.

However, a nuclear bomb needs to be transported to the target and proliferation states develop missiles as 'concomitant technology'.

In addition to the radioactivity, experts are more and more concerned about to the **electromagnetic pulse (EMP)** that can result from a nuclear explosion, because there is an increasing dependency on internet and telecommunication that would be massively damaged by an EMP.

For terrorists, '**dirty bombs**' are of interest, this is to spread radioactive material by an explosion of a huge bomb. But experts believe that such a bomb could only damage relatively small areas which could be cleaned later on again (**decontamination**).

Biologic weapons are e.g. aggressive bacteria or viruses that cause serious infections. From a technical point of view, such a weapon should be easy to prepare, infectious and harmful. However, this is difficult to achieve, lot of preparation steps are necessary that may allow identifying the producing laboratory later on.

The European Medical Agency 2002 has released a paper on bioterrorism in 2002 (updated 2007) that gives useful tips for treatment of infections caused by such weapons.

Some authors are concerned that biotechnology may allow the production of new genetically engineered bacteria and viruses, but this seems also more difficult than expected. However, experts suggest that e.g. laboratories that produce synthetic DNA should be closely supervised.

Another issue is the so-called '**ethnic bomb**', i.e. a bioweapon that only kills certain people. There are some genetic markers that help to identify the ethnic origin in many cases, but none of these variants allows constructing such a selective weapon.

There are many different chemical weapons, but in history gas weapons that damage the neuromuscular system like **Sarin** were most frequently used. As for dirty bombs and bioweapons, it is difficult to control the influence of weather on dissemination and only limited areas may be affected.

However, everybody who plans to use any kind of WMD has to be aware that this may lead to massive retaliation by the attacked countries.

Terrorism is a method, not an ideology, because it was used in history by many radical groups already. This is based on the Latin word terror (anxiety and horror) and terrorism tries to achieve political goals by threats or violence against people and/or things.

These changes may include drawing public attention to the political claims of the terrorists, to achieve negotiations about something or to eliminate political opponents.

However, terrorism is a multi-level phenomenon, e.g. there are globally acting groups such as **Al-Qaeda** ('the basis'), locally acting groups and also **home grown terrorists**, i.e. people attack the country where there were born.

Sometimes, other actors may be involved, and it may be unclear whether a group can be defined as 'terrorists' or as 'rebels', e.g. Ethiopia and Eritrea accuse each other to make a 'proxy war' in Somalia. Moreover, there may be a motive mix. Some groups produce drugs to finance their war, and it may happen that at the end the political goals are more and more replaced by 'business' goals.

Therefore, tailor-made counteractions are necessary, otherwise states may become involved into local conflicts and suddenly they have new allies and enemies that were never on the political agenda. It is massively disputed whether the war in Afghanistan is such a situation.

Organized crime and **piracy** are other global threats, such as the production of and trade with drugs. The problem is that drugs are often very profitable for farmers and dealers and the profits allow a lot of bribery that undermines the war on drugs. Another driver is the high demand, too many people are willing to pay high prices e.g. for cocaine and various types of opiates (heroine and morphine derivates). Main producing countries are Afghanistan for opiates and Colombia for cocaine.

There is a dispute about the **war on drugs**. Some authors argue that without pressure much more drugs would be sold while other believe that there is a **balloon effect**, i.e. if you increase pressure at one point, there will be avoidance reactions (production will be done elsewhere) and the overall drug production was never reduced in history for a longer period.

But what can be done if drugs cannot be eradicated by force? Some authors suggest **legalization**, they argue that the prohibition of alcohol in the US after World War I led to a massively increased crime rate and problems could only stopped by allowing alcohol again. Other argue, that this would damage many people, because at the beginning the intake of drugs may bring good feelings, fitness and fun, but later on, when it is already too late, the health and social life of people is already destroyed.

Piracy was already a problem for the Roman Empire and it is one of the oldest security problems, but this has increased again. Typically, this is located a highly frequented straits e.g. in Africa, Asia and often the pirates know their territory much better than the police and other forces, i.e. this may even be a profitable and sometimes low risk business. This is a danger for the seamen and it leads to increased insurance and transportation costs. Military interventions are discussed as an option, but the coastal states often fear that the real hidden agenda is that foreign nations try to gain control over the sea routes.

Failed States/Asymmetric Wars: After the end of colonialism, the number of unstable or not working states with insufficient institutions (legal system, democratic institutions and procedures) has increased after civil wars. These states are called **failed states**. This is not only a problem due to the lack of democracy and control, but often these states are involved in so-called **asymmetric wars** with unclear or even no fronts, often mix of governmental and non-governmental actors and also a motive-mix.

Some authors believe that states with many resources are much more involved in civil wars, i.e. the resources are the reasons for the civil war. Others argue that resources do not cause civil wars, but help to finance and to prolong them.

However, some authors believe that the failed state theory is too normative and too demanding. In real life, there are no uncontrolled areas, somebody has the control in any case and if you know the right people, you can get everything even in such regions.

These informal structures that also may exist in the background of a failed state are also called '**shadow state**'.

It is also disputed whether **nation building**, i.e. support failed states to build democratic and well-working institutions is a solution. Some authors believe that this is essential for peace keeping while others argue that nation building will never work, if the relevant actors in a region do not want to cooperate.

Limited energy and other resources were already discussed in Sections 4.4.2 and 4.4.3.

There are disputes about the extent and future development of the **climate change**, but the melting of the ice caps clearly indicates that this is a serious matter in progress. The climate change has many implications for security.

In the Arctic region the **North Western sea route** will be more and more passable and Canada is concerned with regard to the expected sea traffic. Some states argue that this will be an international route while Canada claims that this is part of the Canadian territory. As already described, climate change may give new options to exploit resources in the Arctic region.

The expected **increase of the mean sea level** may overflow pacific islands and that would destroy several pacific states like Tuvalu. But as mentioned above, the international community is still not willing to agree upon a legally binding climate treaty (failure of the Copenhagen conference). However, this overflow may also affect other countries, e.g. the Netherlands in Europe and Bangladesh in Asia.

A special topic is water, one example is given here: Many experts expect a **drying-up** of the Gulf Peninsula states starting in 2016, because they need more fresh water than the natural sources can provide in the long run. Some authors believe that this can be solved by **desalinization** of ocean water, but other argue that this is unrealistic, because how should this water transported to the central regions of the countries in an economic manner?

However, the globally increased average temperature could increase migration (**climate refugees**) in many regions of the world.

Demographic problems are observed in many countries. In the Southern hemisphere many governments have to manage fast growing populations, while aging populations are a problem in the Northern hemisphere.

The relative proportion of Europeans is declining and some authors believe that the political power of the Europe Union will be remarkably reduced in the future. Moreover, the population of the Russian Federation is shrinking and the regions east of the Ural Mountains are more and more 'empty' with a few million people on millions of square kilometers. Russian authors are concerned that large parts of Russia may have a Chinese and/or Muslim majority in 2050.

But China also has an aging society and has stopped the '**one child policy**' for population control in some regions. The population of the neighbor state India is much younger.

The demographic situation in the USA is better than in Europe and a further growth of the population is expected, but the structure may change. There is a permanent increase of the Hispanic population in USA and experts believe that in the near future Asians may become third largest group.

Digital technology

Modern societies are increasingly dependent from digital technologies such as computers, mobile phones, and internet and so on. Many computers are connected via internet and the most attacks are executed via internet (in former times by disks), therefore internet security and also computer security are more and more the same. There are three potential weak points: humans, computers and the networks. Relevant threats are:

- Intrusion to collect passwords or other information (**spyware** crime) by **malware** ('Viruses', Worms', 'Trojans' etc.)
- Surveillance of computers to control users (=> marketing!)
- illegal control other computers for illegal purposes (so-called **bot nets**)
- Laptop theft, betray users by **social engineering**
- Attack networks or parts of the internet by **Denial of Service DoS** attacks (overload of computers by senseless requests may lead to network collapse)
- Attack **critical infrastructures** such as government computers, banking systems, electricity nets, military systems
- Abuse of internet (wide range: file sharing networks, children pornography, extremism up to terrorism)

The combination of digital technologies is in progress (e.g. smart phones, Voice over IP etc., sometimes called **Next Generation Network**) and may create new threats. The same is true for the planned **Internet of Things** (IoT), where devices get an internet address, to control, service, and repair and locate them. More and more administrations rely on internet-based communication also known as **e-government**.

Meanwhile, authorities report a broad range of threats (commercial motives up to terrorism) and also that private spyware and supervision capacities are much more efficient.

Things are complicated, because control and supervision may also have legitimate concerns such as an audit trail in research or the **Digital Rights Management** DRM where content providers check the legal use of their products. Sometimes thorough control and documentation may even protect you in legal conflicts where you can provide email as written evidence for your position (so-called **ediscovery** procedure in US civil law).

From a military perspective, a computer attack can start from everywhere and in particular, protection of critical infrastructures necessary. This is why several states build up **cyberwar** units now.

In summary, many authors argue that security policy will be more and more complex, because the number of possible threats and of involved actors is increasing.

What can be done?

The standard suggestion is to enhance cooperation between authorities, information exchange between all types and levels, i.e. between secret services, secret services and other security agencies (police, customs authorities) and to enhance international cooperation as well.

Cooperation can mean organizational and/or financial support and the common collection and exchange of information, e.g. by new databases. Also, coordination centers and coordinators maybe established.

There are concerns that there has to be a **balance between security and privacy**, i.e. human rights need to be respected and the appropriateness of actions needs to be carefully controlled.

Some authors also discussed the structure of security organization. One secret service for everything may sound like a simple solution, but there are concerns that such an organization would be uncontrollable by government. Moreover, if somebody would be able to infiltrate this, too many things would be disclosed. Finally, such an organization may be too large for effective communication and may have **blind spots** (the organization is only focused on danger x, but danger y is the real threat).

Moreover, civil, military and economic issues may be mixed in a service for everything and this may cause a lot of trouble later on.

Due to this reason, the typical solution is to have an **intelligence community**, i.e. a number of services with separate responsibilities but with some kind of coordination and information exchange. Some authors are concerned that the communication exchange may be too cumbersome and that multiple services may compete, interfere or overlap, so it is difficult to find the right size and number of services.

In international cooperation, four rules are essential:

- Do ut des - if you give something, the other one has to give something, too
- Need to know - only necessary information is provided, this is also important if the organization is infiltrated or agents are captured by somebody else
- Third party rule - if you got an information from somebody else, you have to ask before you give information to third parties

- Assessed intelligence - do not provide raw data, otherwise the others may know your methods and may even be able to identify your sources.

While most authors argue that this way of information exchange is effective and rational, some believe that the flow of information is too slow in case of urgent issues. But there needs to be a balance between fast communication and confidentiality.

From a military perspective, armies were transformed after the end of cold war from large units to smaller and more flexible and mobile units such as quick reaction forces.

Most military missions are currently done as missions of the UNO, by the NATO or as US and European military missions.

Some authors discuss a whether there is a **responsibility to protect (R2P)**, i.e. the need and the right for a foreign intervention if the local government is not able or willing to protect their people in critical situations. Some authors argue that such a concept is not covered by the law of nations while others believe that this approach may overstretch military and political capacities of the democratic states.

6. Conclusion

This short course has shown that Political Science may not be able to provide theories that are true in every situation and often there may be no objective truth in political matters at all.

Nevertheless, Political Science provides a lot of theories and tools that allow a better to understanding and analysis of political matters.

7. Literature

Abels, H. Einführung in die Soziologie in zwei Bänden. In der Reihe von Abels, H, Fuchs-Henritz, W., Jäger, W., Schimank, U. (Hrsg.) Hagener Studientexte zur Soziologie. VS Verlag für Sozialwissenschaften

Albert, Hans (2000): Vier Kapitel zur Kritik illusionären Denkens. Mohr Siebeck Verlag, UTB Taschenbuchausgabe.

Alemann von, U. (2005): Das Parteiensystem der Bundesrepublik Deutschland. Leske und Budrich Verlag.

Alemann von, U., Czada, R. (1998): Kongressbeiträge zur Politischen Soziologie, Politischen Ökonomie und Politikfeldanalyse. Hrsg. Vom Institut für Politikwissenschaft der FernUniversität – Gesamthochschule Hagen- FB Erziehungs-, Sozial- und Geisteswissenschaften, 58084 Hagen polis 39/1998

Bandelow, N.C. (1999): Lernende Politik. Advocacy-Koalitionen und politischer Wandel am Beispiel der Gentechnologiepolitik. Berlin, Edition Sigma.

Bardach, Eugene (2000): A Practical Guide for Policy Analysis. The eightfold path to more effective problem solving. Chatham House Publication, New York.

Barrow, J.D. (1993): Die Natur der Natur: Wissen an den Grenzen von Raum und Zeit. Heidelberg: Spektrum Verlag 1993.

Beck, U. (1986): Risikogesellschaft. Auf dem Weg in eine andere Moderne. Suhrkamp Verlag, Frankfurt im Nachdruck von 2000.

Behrens, M. et al. (2005): Globalisierung als politische Herausforderung. VS Verlag für Sozialwissenschaften.

Benz, A. (2004): Governance - Regieren in komplexen Regelsystemen, Wiesbaden: VS Verlag für Sozialwissenschaften, 2004.

Benz, A., Lütz, S., Schimank, U., Simonis, G. (2007): Handbuch Governance - Theoretische Grundlagen und empirische Anwendungsfelder, Wiesbaden: VS Verlag für Sozialwissenschaften, 2007.

Bertelsmann-Stiftung (1993): Hochschulpolitik im internationalen Vergleich. Verlag Bertelsmann Stiftung, Gütersloh 1993.

Blatter, J., Janning F., Wagemann (2006): Qualitative Politikanalyse. Eine Einführung in Forschungsansätze und Methoden, VS Verlag für Sozialwissenschaften 2007.

Böhret., C., Jann, W, Kronenwett, E. (1988): Innenpolitik und politische Theorie. Westdeutscher Verlag, 3. Auflage.

Bogumil, J., Jann, W. (2005): Einführung in die Verwaltungswissenschaft in Deutschland. VS Verlag für Sozialwissenschaften 2005.

Bogumil, J., Schmid, J. (2002): Politik in Organisationen: Organisationstheoretische Ansätze und praxisbezogene Anwendungsbeispiele, VS Verlag für Sozialwissenschaften 2001.

Bogdandy, A. von (2005): Auswertung der rechtswissenschaftlichen Projekte. In: Mayntz, R., Bogdandy, A. von, Genschel, P. und Lütz, S. (2005): Globale Strukturen und deren Steuerung. Auswertung der Ergebnisse eines Förderprogramms der Volkswagenstiftung. Max-Planck Institut für Gesellschaftsforschung Köln 2005, 177 Seiten: 1-62.

Bredow, W. von (2000): Militär, Staat und Gesellschaft in der Bundesrepublik Deutschland. Westdeutscher Verlag, Hagen 2000

Bundesregierung (2007): Elemente einer Rohstoffstrategie der Bundesregierung. März 2007, 32. S.

Coase, R.H. (1937), The Nature of the Firm, in: Economica 4, S.386-405.

Coase, R.H. (1960), The Problem of Social Cost, in: Journal of Law and Economics, Jg.3, S.1-44.

Czada, R., Schmidt, M.G. (1993) Verhandlungsdemokratie-Interssenvermittlung-Regierbarkeit. Westdeutscher Verlag, Opladen 1993.

Czada, R. (1997): Neuere Entwicklungen der Politikfeldanalyse. Vortrag auf dem Schweizerischen Politologentag am 14. November 1997 in Balsthal:47-66. [Als Internetquelle einsehbar]

Czada, R., Lütz, S. (Hrsg.): Die politische Konstitution von Märkten. Wiesbaden: Westdeutscher Verlag, 2000.

Czada, R., Héritier, A., Keman, H. (eds.): 1998: Institutions and Political Choice. On the limits of rationality. Amsterdam: VU Press, pp. 229-256 (first published 1991, Campus-Verlag, Frankfurt

Czada, R., Lütz, S., Mette: (2003): Regulative Politik. Zähmungen von Markt und Technik. VS Verlag für Sozialwissenschaften.

Dahrendorf, R. (1973): Arbeitsprogramm Forschung, Wissenschaft und Bildung. Wissenschaftliche und technische Information. Brüssel 1973, S.4-9.

Davidow, W.H., Malone, M.S. (1993): Das virtuelle Unternehmen: Der Kunde als Co-Produzent, Frankfurt/Main-New York 1993 (Übersetzung aus dem Englischen).

Döhler; M.; Manow P. (1997): Strukturbildung von Politikfeldern. Das Beispiel bundesdeutscher Gesundheitspolitik seit den fünfziger Jahren. Band 13 der Reihe Gesellschaftspolitik und Staatstätigkeit Leske und Budrich Verlag, Opladen 1997, 198 S.

Eichener, V., Voelzkow, H. (1994): Europäische Integration und verbandliche Interessenvermittlung. Metropolis Verlag, Marburg 1994.

Eising R., FernUniversität in Hagen und Lenschow A., Universität Osnabrück: Governance und politische Steuerung in der Europäischen Union.

Elsner, W. (1984): Ökonomische Institutionenanalyse, in: Volkswirtschaftliche Schriften, Berlin, Heft 367.

Endres, A. (1997): Umweltökonomie, 3. Auflage Kohlhammer Verlag.

Europäisches Regieren. Ein Weissbuch. Kommission der Europäischen Gemeinschaften. Brüssel, den 25.7.2001, KOM(2001) 428 endgültig http://europa.eu.int/comm/governance/governance/index_en.htm

Fach, W. (1999): Die Hüter der Vernunft - Eine Einführung in das Ordnungsdenken Leske + Budrich, 1999.

Fischhoff, B., Lichtenstein, S., Slovic, P., Derby, S.L., Keeney, R.L. (1981): Acceptable Risk. Cambridge University Press 1981, Chapters 1 and 2, p.1-46

Fuchs-Henritz, W., König, A. (2005): Werner Fuchs-Heinritz und Alexandra König: Pierre Bourdieu. Eine Einführung. UVK, Konstanz

94

Furubotn, E.G., Pejovich, S. (1972): Property Rights and Economic Theory: A Survey of Recent Literature, In: The Journal of Economic Literature, Vol.10:1137-1162.

Gäfgen, G. (1984): Entwicklung und Stand der Theorie der Property Rights: Eine kritische Bestandsaufnahme, in: Neumann, M.(Hrsg.) Ansprüche, Eigentums- und Verfügungsrechte, Schriftenreihe des Vereins für Socialpolitik, Band 140, Berlin 1984.

Galtung, J. (2007): Frieden mit friedlichen Mitteln: Frieden, Konflikt, Entwicklung und Kultur. Agenda Verlag.

Gellner, W., Strohmeier, G. (Hrsg.) Freiheit und Gemeinwohl - Politikfelder und Politikvermittlung zu Beginn des 21. Jahrhunderts. Nomos-Verlagsgesellschaft 2002

Goldthau, A. (2008): Rhetoric versus reality: Russian threats to European energy supply. In: Energy Policy 36 (2008) 686-692

Hasse, R, Krücken, G. (2005): Der Neue Institutionalismus. Transcript Verlag.,

Hein, W. (1996): Unterentwicklung - Krise der Peripherie, Opladen 1998.

Hellmann, G. (2006): Deutsche Außenpolitik. Verlag für Sozialwissenschaften.

Holzer, V.L. (2006): Europäische und deutsche Energiepolitik. Europäische Schriften zu Staat und Wirtschaft. Nomos Verlag, Band 22.

Hèretier, A. (1995): Die Koordination von Interessenvielfalt im europäischen Entscheidungsprozess und deren Ergebnis: Regulative Politik als "Patchwork". MPIfG Discussion Paper 95/2 des MPIfG = Max-Planck-Institut für Gesellschaftsforschung:1-29.

Heinrichs, W. (1997): Kulturpolitik und Kulturfinanzierung, Beck Juristischer.

Henning, F.W. (1995): Die Industrialisierung in Deutschland 1800-1914, 9.Auflage, Schöningh Verlag, 308 Seiten.

Honneth, A. (2006): Schlüsseltexte der Kritischen Theorie. VS Verlag für Sozialwissenschaften, Wiesbaden 2006.

Jachtenfuchs, M; Kohler-Koch, B. (1996): Europäische Integration. Leske + Budrich Verlag, Opladen, 1996

Jäger, W., Weinzierl, U. (2007): Moderne soziologische Theorien und sozialer Wandel. Verlag für Sozialwissenschaften.

Jaschke, H.G. (1991): Streitbare Demokratie und innere Sicherheit. Grundlagen, Praxis und Kritik. Leske und Budrich Verlag, Opladen 1991

Kant, Immanuel (1998): Kritik der reinen Vernunft. Nach der ersten und zweiten Originalausgabe 1781/1787. 1998 neu herausgegeben von Jens Timmermann. Felix Meiner-Philosophische Bibliothek 505, Hamburg 1998, 995 S.

Kleinfeld, R. (1996): Kommunalpolitik. Leske und Budrich Verlag.

Kohler-Koch, B. (1992): Interessen und Integration. Die Rolle organisierter Interessen im westeuropäischen Integrationsprozeß. In: Politische Vierteljahresschrift, 33 Jg., Sonderheft 23/1992:81-119.

Kohler-Koch, B. (1996): Europäische Integration. Leske + Budrich Verlag, Opladen, 1996:225-248.

Kohler-Koch, B.; Conzelmann, Th., Knodt, M. (2004): Europäische Integration - Europäisches Regieren. Verlag für Sozialwissenschaften ISBN-10: 3810035432.

Kropp, S. (2007): Kooperativer Föderalismus und Politikverflechtung. Verlag für Sozialwissenschaften.

Lange, S., Schimank, U. (2004): Governance und gesellschaftliche Integration. Verlag für Sozialwissenschaften.

Leibfried, S., Pierson, P. (1999): European Social Policy. In: ZeS-Arbeitspapier 15/1999 des Zentrums für Sozialpolitik, Univ. Bremen, 41 S.

List, M., Reichhardt, W., Simonis, G. (1995): Internationale Politik - Probleme und Grundbegriffe. VS Verlag für Sozialwissenschaften; Auflage: 1 (1995).

Lütz, S. (1998): Wenn Banken sich vergessen. Risikoregulierung im internationalen Mehr-Ebenen-System. MPIfG Discussion Paper 98/5 des MPIfG = Max-Planck-Institut für Gesellschaftsforschung, 32 S.

Lütz, S. (2006): Governance in der politischen Ökonomie. VS Verlag für Sozialwissenschaften.

Mäder, W. (1994): Bausteine Europas: Integrations- und Gesundheitspolitik der europäischen Gemeinschaft. Dümmler Verlag Bonn 1994, 206.S.

Mayntz, R. (1993): Gemeinwohl und Ärzteinteressen - die Politik des Hartmannbundes. Gütersloh

Mayntz, R. (1997): Soziale Dynamik und politische Steuerung. Theoretische und methodologische Überlegungen. Campus-Verlag, 340 S.

Mayntz, R., Bogdandy, A. von, Genschel, P. und Lütz, S. (2005): Globale Strukturen und deren Steuerung. Auswertung der Ergebnisse eines Förderprogramms der Volkswagenstiftung. Max-Planck. Institut für Gesellschaftsforschung Köln 2005, 177 S. (Im Internet erhältlich)

In: Müller, H.P.: Sozialer Wandel. Frankfurt 1995.

Müller, F. (2004): Klimapolitik und Energieversorgungssicherheit. Zwei Seiten derselben Medaille. Studie S14 der Stiftung Wissenschaft und Politik (SWP) April 2004, Berlin 2004

Müller, R.A. (1996): Geschichte der Universität. Von der mittelalterlichen Universitas zur deutschen Hochschule, Nikol Verlag, 288 Seiten.

Naschold F. (1993): Modernisierung des Staates. Zur Ordnungs- und Innovationspolitik des öffentlichen Sektors, Berlin 1993

Nipperdey, Th. (1994): Deutsche Geschichte 1800-1866. Bürgerwelt und starker Staat, C.H. Beck Verlag, München, 838 Seiten.

Nohlen/Schultze (Hrsg.) 1995: Lexikon der Politik, Bd.I, München: Beck-Verlag

North, M. (2000): Deutsche Wirtschaftsgeschichte. Ein Jahrtausend im Überblick. C.H. Beck Verlag.

Nuffield Council (2002a): Genetics and human behaviour – the ethical context. Published by Nuffield Council on Bioethics, October 2002, 213 S.

Nuffield Council (2002): The ethics of patenting DNA – a discussion paper of the ethical context. Published by Nuffield Council on Bioethics, October 2002.

Parsons, W. (1995): Public Policy: An introduction to the Theory and Practice of Policy Analysis. Lyme, CT: Edward Elgar Press.

Prittwitz, V.w. (1994): Politikanalyse. Leske+Budrich, Opladen.

Popper, Karl (2003): Die offene Gesellschaft und ihre Feinde. Mohr Siebeck Verlag, Band 1, 524 S. mit 29 Seiten Vorwort zu den deutschen Auflagen (S.I-XXIX) und Band 2, 575 S.

Popper, Karl (2005): Logik der Forschung. Mohr Siebeck Verlag, 11. Auflage, 601 S. mit 37 Seiten Vorwort zu den deutschen Auflagen (S.I-XXXVII)

Rásky, B. (1997) Kulturpolitik(en) in Europa - die nationalstaatlichen Rahmenbedingungen. Hrsg.: Ellmeier, A.; Rásky, B. (1997): Kulturpolitik in Europa - Europäische Kulturpolitik? Kultur-dokumentation des Internationalen Archivs für Kulturanalysen. Wien 1997, S.1-106.

Rawls, John (1994): Eine Theorie der Gerechtigkeit. Übersetzung von H. Vetter. 8. Auflage, Frankfurt am Main 1994, 688 S.

Reiche, D. (2005): Grundlagen der Energiepolitik. Peter Lang Verlag, 330 S.

Richter, R. (1987), Geldtheorie: Eine Vorlesung auf der Grundlage der Allgemeinen Gleichgewichtstheorie und der Institutionenökonomik, Berlin-Heidelberg-New York.

Rieger, E.; Leibfried: (1997): Die sozialpolitischen Grenzen der Globalisierung. In: PVS, 38.Jg.:771-796.

Rittberger, V. (2003). Internationale Organisationen: Politik und Geschichte. Verlag für Sozialwissenschaften.

Rudzio, W. (2006): Das politische System der Bundesrepublik Deutschland. Verlag für Sozialwissenschaften.

Scharpf, F.W. (1985): Die Politikverflechtungs-Falle. Europäische Integration und deutscher Föderalismus im Vergleich. In: PVS, 26.Jg., H.4:323-356.

Scharpf, F.W. (1992): Versuch über Demokratie in Verhandlungssystemen. MPIfG Discussion Paper 92/9 des MPIfG = Max-Planck-Institut für Gesellschaftsforschung.

Scharpf, F.W. (1997): Balancing Positive and Negative Integration. The Regulatory Options for Europe. MPIfG Working Paper 97/8.

Scharpf, F.W. (2000): Interaktionsformen: Akteurzentrierter Institutionalismus in der Politikforschung. UTB für Wissenschaft bei Leske+Budrich, Opladen.

Scharpf, F.W. (2002): MPIfG Working Paper 02/8, July 2002. The European Social Model: Coping with the Challenges of Diversity.

Schenk, K.E. (1992), Die Neue Institutionenökonomie- ein Überblick über wichtige Elemente und Probleme der Weiterentwicklung, in: Zeitschrift für Wirtschafts- und Sozialwissenschaften, Vol.112(3), S.339-372.

Schimank, U. (2007): Theorien gesellschaftlicher Differenzierung. Verlag für Sozialwissenschaften.

Schmidt, M.G. (1995): Demokratietheorien. Eine Einführung. Opladen 1995.

Schmidt, M.G.: Sozialpolitik in Deutschland. Historische Entwicklung und internationaler Vergleich.

Schmidt, M.G. (1997): Policy-Analyse. In: Mohr, A. (1997): Grundzüge der Politikwissenschaft, S.567-605. Lehr- und Handbücher der Politikwissenschaft, Oldenbourg Verlag 1997, 2. Auflage.

Schneider, H. (1992): Europäische Integration: die Leitbilder und die Politik. In: Politische Vierteljahresschrift, 33 Jg., Sonderheft 23/1992:3-35.

Schreyögg, G. (1994): Umwelt, Technologie und Organisationsstruktur: Eine Analyse des kontingenztheoretischen Ansatzes, 2.Auflage, Bern-Stuttgart-Wien 1994.

Schubert, K., Bandelow, N. (2003): Lehrbuch der Politikfeldanalyse. Lehr- und Handbücher der Politikwissenschaft, Oldenbourg Verlag 2003.

Schulze, G. (1995): Die Erlebnisgesellschaft –Kultursoziologie der Gegenwart. Campus Verlag, 5. Auflage, Frankfurt-New York, S.54ff..

Simon, H.A. (1984), On The Behavioral And Rational Foundations Of Economic Dynamics, in: Journal of Economic Behaviour and Organization, Vol.5, S.35-55.

Simonis, G., Martinsen, R. und Saretzki, T. (Hrsg.) Politik und Technik. Analysen zum Verhältnis von technologischem, politischem und staatlichen Wandel am Anfang des 21. Jahrhunderts. Deutsche Vereinigung für Politische Wissenschaft, Westdeutscher Verlag, 1. Auflage.

Tömmel, I. (2003): Das politische System der EU. Oldenbourg Verlag, München, 2003.

Van der Linde, C. (2007): External energy policy: old fears and new dilemmas in a larger Union. In: Fragmented Power: Europe and the Global Economy, Chapter 9, 266-307. Edited by André Sapir, Bruegel Books, Brussels 2007.

Voelzkow, H. (1996): Private Regierungen in der Techniksteuerung. Eine sozialwissenschaftliche Analyse der technischen Normung. Campus Verlag.

Wagner, H. (2000): Europäische Wirtschaftspolitik - Perspektiven einer europäischen Wirtschafts- und Währungsunion (EWWU). Springer Verlag.

Werle, R./ Schimank, U.: Gesellschaftliche Komplexität und kollektive Handlungsfähigkeit. Frankfurt a.M.: Campus, 2000.

Williamson, O.E. (1975), Markets and Hierarchies: Analysis and Antitrust Implications, London-New York 1975.

Williamson, O.E. (1989), Transaction Cost Economics, in: Handbook of Industrial Organization, Volume I, Edited by R. Schmalensee and R.D. Willig.

Zimmer. A. (1996): Vereine - Basiselemente der Demokratie. Eine Analyse aus der Dritte-Sektor-Perspektive. Leske + Budrich, Opladen 1996.